How Far Down Does the Elephant Go?

How Far Down Does the Elephant Go?

Unfinished Conversations with My High School Students

Hugh P. Kemp

RESOURCE *Publications* • Eugene, Oregon

HOW FAR DOWN DOES THE ELEPHANT GO?
Unfinished Conversations with My High School Students

Copyright © 2024 Hugh P. Kemp. All rights reserved. Except for brief quotations in critical publications or reviews, no part of this book may be reproduced in any manner without prior written permission from the publisher. Write: Permissions, Wipf and Stock Publishers, 199 W. 8th Ave., Suite 3, Eugene, OR 97401.

Resource Publications
An Imprint of Wipf and Stock Publishers
199 W. 8th Ave., Suite 3
Eugene, OR 97401

www.wipfandstock.com

PAPERBACK ISBN: 979-8-3852-0960-6
HARDCOVER ISBN: 979-8-3852-0961-3
EBOOK ISBN: 979-8-3852-0962-0

VERSION NUMBER 05/07/24

For my students in the classes of 2023 and 2024
at Saint Kentigern College, Auckland.
Thanks for pushing back with the hard questions.
May we all continue to grow in the direction of our questions.

There is no greater agony than bearing an untold story inside you.
—Maya Angelou

Child, to say the very thing you really mean, the whole of it, nothing more or less or other than what you really mean, that's the whole art and joy of words.
—C.S. Lewis

It is not from ourselves that we learn to be better than we are.
—Wendell Berry

Contents

Preface | ix

1. "How far down does the elephant go?" | 1
2. "Are you actually serious when you claim that Jesus rose from the dead?" | 6
3. "Knowing stuff—how do you know what you claim is true?" | 13
4. "Do you really think God actually created the world in seven literal days?" | 24
5. "If God is so good, then why is there evil in the world?" | 31
6. "What is the right thing to do, and why should I do it?" | 39
7. "How would you recognize a Christian?" | 49
8. "Can we really know what (your Christian) God is like?" | 58
9. "Why are there so many different religions in the world?" | 67
10. "Isn't it all just 'meant to be'?" | 83
11. "If God can do anything, then why doesn't he just fix stuff, like world hunger" and "What's this word 'shalom' you use all the time?" | 93

Preface

This book is the product of eight years wrestling with the big questions my students have asked.

Between 2015 and 2023, I taught at Saint Kentigern College in Auckland, New Zealand. Saint Kentigern College is a private "church school"—Presbyterian—a combined Middle School and High School of about 2,200 students. The college offers the New Zealand curriculum—the National Certificate of Educational Achievement (NCEA)—and it also offers the International Baccalaureate Diploma (IB). I shared my teaching equally between Christian Education (CE) and a course called *Theory of Knowledge* (TOK). Christian Education was compulsory for all students but was not part of either curriculum: we had designed our own courses. Theory of Knowledge, on the other hand, is a core course in the IB Diploma and taught in all IB World Schools globally. I tended to teach senior students. Most of my classes were Years 11—13 (ages 15–17), but some years I'd have one or two year 9 CE classes (13 year olds).

Teaching CE and TOK, my days were full of big questions. I like to think I modelled myself on Socrates, striving for provocative open ended questions, rather than simply dishing up propositional claims. I was committed to an enquiry strategy, introducing students to ways of thinking and learning, rather than just raw content. I wanted to encourage students to embrace a critical stance with me acting as a kind of optometrist of knowledge, adjusting their lenses, cleaning and polishing them when appropriate, and always encouraging students to seek a clear vision of the world. Some days I'd lob a curling question and the lesson looked after itself where fresh ideas were examined and assumptions critiqued. Other times, we could barely see for the mud and blood on the lenses.

In all senior classes, somewhere in the year, I'd either have a question box or some other mechanism to elicit students' broader questions, those questions which drifted around the edges of the syllabus: "drop your question—any questions at all—into the box. We will mix them all up and start pulling them out and we'll see where the conversation goes". In one unit in Year 11, students wrote their questions on Postit stickers and stuck them all over the whiteboard. A volunteer would then choose the questions for that period. It was all a bit scary: I committed to addressing every question, no matter how pertinent, relevant, inane, marginal, diverse or sexual it was. At the beginning of most days, I had little idea of how the day might end. For me, my classes were both terrifying and exhilarating. They stretched me as much as I hoped they would challenge the students. All questions had to be managed with great pastoral sensitivity. For many questions, we barely got started: so many were left unanswered, or only partially answered, or incomprehensibly answered, which was usually my fault for not listening well enough.

Many days I'd end up sitting on the deck—interval, recess, lunchtime, before and after school—shooting the breeze with a student or two, continuing the class discussions, exploring issues of life, faith, hope, dreams, God, karma, plans, relationships, religion, careers and pretty much anything students wanted to talk about. On the deck, literally. I had a wooden deck—a veranda—running around my classroom with benches on it. This was often the most lucid time of my day. One student, four years after he graduated, told me that conversations with me sitting on the deck at lunchtime eating our sandwiches and enjoying the warmth of the spring sunshine was the highlight of his time at High School. I never knew. Students expected me to talk about Jesus because, after all, I was a Christian Education teacher. Students expected me to dig deep and be at home with philosophical enquiry because, after all, I was also an epistemology teacher. And they all expected me to be available. Which I was quite happy to be.

But so many conversations were started and not finished: so many questions were pulled from the box and still lie on the table. This book is an attempt to try and complete some conversations, or at least keep them moving. I've shaped the conversations as letters. I hope that even though so much of life is now dominated by social media genres, readers will still appreciate a letter. If you're one of my ex-students, you may recognize the conversation, or something close to it, or recognize the lesson that it drops out of. If you haven't been one of my students, then welcome to the conversation! Take time to read, ponder, and keep the conversation going. Carpe diem!

I've tried to imagine how this book might be used. The simple joy of conversation needs no justification. But I think it could be used as a reader for youth groups. If there are church youth groups or book clubs or philosophy or debating groups who want to tackle these deeper questions, then this book could be a resource: an astute youth group leader could design questions for each chapter for further discussions; an innovative moderator could precipitate a proposition for debate. I'd like to think that this book might make its way back into High Schools. Maybe CE and Religious Education teachers could use it as a set text, or maybe chaplains could use it to help students who continue to wrestle with these questions.

All the names I've chosen are random. Well not really. As a teacher, I have to know about 300 names at any one time, and some names belong to more than one individual. One year I had two students with the name "Ocean" in the same class. What are the odds of that? I simply can't help but use names that are real names of students I have recently taught. If you recognize a name (or you recognize your own name), then consider it coincidence. The conversations are real, and they happened (or have started). All questions were generated by the students themselves. I'm not saying they should or shouldn't be asking these or any other questions. These are theirs. But whether with the named recipient or not is a moot point.

Preface

In writing up these conversations, I have the actual conversation partner in mind, but for privacy reasons have changed the name. If you're one of my students reading this and you recognize yourself, then that is serendipitous only and not intentional.

A huge thanks to my students who have had the courage to ask these questions! And a special thanks to Ally Stuant—a Year 12 student—who was the first to read the text in one sitting and affirm that this book is a worthwhile project.

I have also so appreciated the culture of enquiry that Saint Kentigern College has facilitated, allowing the teachers in the CE department a generous context to explore these big questions with their students. A special shout-out to Jeremy Sievers, Head of Christian Education, Suzie Tornquist, Head of IB, and Duncan McQueen, Director of Campus Life and Special Character for their professional and personal support in this incredible journey with my amazing students. *Fides Servanda Est.*

1

"How far down does the elephant go?"

Vicki,

I know, I know. This question was actually mine, but you guys have taken great delight this year in parroting it as a sort of class mantra because I repeated it so often, and because so much is determined by how we answer this question. "How far down does the elephant go?" Another class shaped the question as "what's the elephant standing on"?

I hope you were able to follow the story well enough in class? It's a story called *The Four Friends* and you find it throughout Asia in various forms. Four friends—a partridge, a hare, a monkey and an elephant—were out in the forest and they saw some juicy looking fruit hanging high in a tree, but out of reach. The story is about friendship (they all co-operated and worked out together how to reach the fruit), but I've used the story with my classes as a way to raise the question about assumptions. I keep challenging you guys about your pre-conceived ideas, what you're bringing to the table. What are your assumptions? Where do you get them from? Why do you hold to them? Do you realize you have them? The question has become our mantra.

How Far Down Does the Elephant Go?

So, here's the gist of the story again. Picture a parent—OK, I'm male, so father—reading the story to his five year old daughter. (I have daughters.) You can imagine snuggling up in bed and finishing the story: ".... and so because they co-operated with each other, the partridge was able to reach the fruit which they shared and all enjoyed. End of story. Good night". Kiss, hug, and into bed.

"But wait", my daughter says. "How did the partridge reach that high? What was the partridge standing on?"

"On the shoulders of the hare", I reply.

"And what was the hare standing on?", she continues.

"On the shoulders of the monkey".

Imagining a descending sequence of getting-bigger animal friends now forming a stable tower, she then asks "and what's the monkey standing on?"

"On the shoulders of the elephant", I reply patiently. But I know what's coming.

"And so, Daddy, what's the elephant standing on?", she finally asks.

By this time I'm frustrated and bored with the story and say "I don't know ... he's just ... ."

She interrupts, now imagining an extending column downward of some sort: "Daddy, daddy. How far down does the elephant go?"

And that Vicki, is the question. I've been using it as a metaphor, a philosophical device to challenge us about the very assumptions that we stand on. About the fundamental ideas that we don't name but on which we build a huge edifice, like the tower of co-operating friends in the story, so as to reach the fruit. The foundations—the whatever-stuff the elephant is standing on—are the axioms, the unexamined assumptions that we hold to, rarely name, but are simply there. If we change "what's the elephant standing on" to "how far down does the elephant go", then this prompts us to think about regresses. That's when we ask a question like "who made God?", and answer it "well, there must have been another god who was bigger". And so who made that god, well another one, and on and on and on back ("regress") into the infinite past. How far down does that elephant go? Is there anything at all that the elephant is standing on?

We have to start from somewhere. We have to build on something. And that starting point cannot be proved or explained: it's just accepted. I can think of two examples which might illustrate this. Think of the Greek mathematician/philosopher we studied in class: Euclid. One of Euclid's axioms is "the shortest distance between two points is a straight line". D'oh. Of course. Well, that's the point. It's so obvious, we don't have to even name it. But did Euclid "prove" this mathematically? No. He just accepts it—it's a starting place, an axiom. And then on that axiom (and a few others)—all such obvious claims—he (and we) built the discipline of Geometry. Another one might be that famous statement in the American Declaration of Independence: "we hold these truths to be self-evident, that all men are created equal . . ." The other truths it then goes on to name are "self-evident": these just are, no one has to prove them; we all accept them. It's what the elephant is standing on.

So when we're debating something in class, and we suspect a claim is being made without examination of the assumptions behind it, we've been using this question: "how far down does the elephant go"? In other words, how did you arrive at that conclusion? What bias do you have? What are you assuming here? What fundamental givens have you accepted without being aware of them? What do you need to go and re-examine to make sure your foundations are steady? Or to put it another way: what's your elephant standing on?

I get the question "who created God?" every year, usually from Year 11 students who I suspect are trying to catch me out with a deep philosophical enquiry that they think will tie me up in knots. It is that infinite regression: "who made god"? Answer: a bigger god. If pushed, I suppose you could allow for an infinite regression (would that allow for reincarnation?), but I think we compromise meaningful discussion there because we'd end up in an infinite loop, perhaps. But we could think of that regression like a line of causes: everything in the universe is caused by something else. You can take the line of causation back and back and back. We talked about this in one of my classes. How far back can we take it? What was the first cause that triggered everything else? How far down does this elephant go? What's this elephant standing on? The Christian claim is that there is a beginning: there is one un-caused entity in the universe. This is another axiom. It's a claim, but not proven, or provable. Like Euclid's axioms, or the "self-evidence" of the founding fathers of America, it just is. It's a given. It's a starting point that is un-provable. I choose to see the starting point of everything in the world as an un-caused entity. Yes? No? I'd be interested to know what you think.

There is no argument for or against the existence of this un-caused entity, but if we change this up now into more Christian language, we'd be talking about God. God is the first and only un-caused entity in the universe. God is, and God caused everything else to happen in some way. The Bible doesn't try and justify or prove the existence of God: it assumes the existence of God. The Bible simply starts: "In the beginning God created . . ." If you consolidate the Bible's teaching on God's creating, we say that God created *ex-nihilo*, that is, out of nothing. If you dig deeper, the Bible claims that God creates by speaking things into existence.

I think we should note that we all carry assumptions about how we see the world. Do you think this would be true? We carry a basketful of unproven (and often un-provable) givens about how we see life, and what the nature of reality is, and who we are, and what are our possibilities and the likes. And for meaningful discussion to happen about these big questions, we need to first acknowledge that we do hold to some axioms. In some sense they are beyond reason: they just are, and we just hold them. Perhaps then we start with faith, that is, believing that we can still have meaningful discussions about big questions because we acknowledge that the elephant is standing on something, even if we're not quite sure how far down the elephant goes.

I'm able to name two assumptions my own elephant is standing on. Firstly, this is an open universe. I think I'm consistent with science on this: no law in the universe is set in concrete. The universe is not a Newtonian machine. The scientific method gives conditional and pragmatic truths—our laws of the universe describe what normally happens most of the time. But not all the time. You can't guarantee 100% that the sun will come up tomorrow. If the universe is indeed open, then this allows miracles to happen, where miracles would be intentional intervention by God. (A theological argument here is that if God created this universe, then surely God has every right to tweak it, fiddle with it, step in and out of it, and intervene in it. Does the potter not have the right to shape the clay as she wishes? A side note though: the Bible also tells us that God is constant, reliable, unchangeable and not fickle.) My second assumption is that God exists. I'm not defining this God at this moment (I'd go on to say that this God is the one who reveals God-self in the Bible), but when I say that one of my axioms is "God exists"—I nor you can actually prove that. But then I or you cannot prove that God doesn't exist either. Or, that only one God exists and not many. But we have to start somewhere. Maybe what follows after identifying an axiom is then to set up some If-Then scenarios, to use our imaginations to see what shape our knowledge might take. Here's one: "If God exists, then is the Bible the best way for God to show God-self to us?" And away we'd go with a good discussion.

One of the challenges in life is to ask ourselves if we live our lives consistent with our assumptions. Will what the elephant is standing on be solid and stable enough to have our friends stand on our shoulders to build a tower to reach the delicious fruit? It's all very well to preface the Declaration of Independence with "it is self-evident that all men are equal . . .", but do we actually live as if that's true? There is class, caste, exploitation, slavery, which would bely this claim. That's why it's important to recognize that our behaviors—our ethics, how we live—are so important. Maybe the question shifts to: "how consistent am I in behaving in ways that match my axioms and beliefs?" That question itself bubbles under the surface of much of what follows in these letters. Look out for it, and keep asking yourself "how far down does the elephant go?".

Shalom, Mr Kemp.

2

"Are you actually serious when you claim that Jesus rose from the dead?"

Jack,

You seemed quite incredulous in class today about my conviction that Jesus actually rose from the dead. I know it sounds a bit preposterous. From your experience—and mine too—you (or I) have never seen anyone or heard about anyone actually coming back to life these days. (Well I have—but that's for another day when we might talk about miracles, and that will be about resuscitation, not resurrection, and there's a difference. But I'm digressing.) At best we might see a doctor in a TV show use the defib paddles to "bring someone back to life". "A miracle", someone on the show declares, as the heartbeat starts oscillating on the monitor and we all exhale our tension of the moment.

But like I said in class, my whole Christian faith really hangs on this resurrection-of-Jesus claim. And to make as outrageous a claim as this, I better have some good evidence. A claim has to be justified, and a bold claim has to be justified even more, with both quantity and quality of evidence. I hope you'd expect nothing less!

I concede it did sound a bit trite when I announced in class that I believe Jesus rose from the dead because I talked to him this morning. The class was right to push back and question my subjective experience. Can we allow personal testimony into a debate that claims to be evidence-based and rational? I do think that personal testimony—subjective experience—is admissible. The burden of proof then shifts away from the content—the truth claim—of what's said, over to the character of the speaker. In a court of law, personal testimony is admitted all the time, and the reliability of the witness, the character of the person, gives that testimony weight (or not).

C.S. Lewis captures this well in that scene in *The Lion, The Witch and the Wardrobe* (and I'm so relieved that most of your generation is familiar with the film, if not the books), where Peter and Susan go to the Professor Digory Kirke and describe their sister Lucy's apparently outrageous claim that there is a land on the other side of the wardrobe. The professor leans forward and, looking over the top of his glasses while puffing his pipe, says something like "well if Lucy is not mad, and she's not lying, then logically we must assume she's telling the truth." In other words, if you know she is trustworthy—her character—then why not concede that something extraordinary, something out of this world, has indeed happened, even if (particularly if) it threatens the very view of reality we hold? He challenges their worldview, their assumptions about the nature of reality, because Lucy proposed it, and Lucy is trustworthy, and Peter and Susan have always experienced Lucy as trustworthy.

So when I say "I spoke to the (risen) Jesus this morning", you know it's an outrageous claim, but I sensed you didn't quite know what to make of it. So the professor's question comes to us: am I trustworthy? And do you experience me as trustworthy? Would I be trying to deceive you? And if so, why? You know I do have you guys on a bit—I love a good laugh and we have some funny moments in class. However, I'm not one to joke about something so weighty. It's your call about my claim. And I hope my character is trustworthy, and my professional standing—I am your teacher, after all—would give you confidence to consider the claim at least. It requires courage to consider a claim that is shaped by a completely different worldview than your own. Peter and Susan are perplexed, but they do find ultimately that Lucy was indeed telling the truth.

I wasn't actually surprized when Olivia jumped in and asked "well what did Jesus say to you?" This question always follows when I make this statement in any class I have. I just wait, and someone inevitably asks it. I liked this interjection because it implies that Olivia conceded that talking to an alive-again Jesus might be possible, and besides, how would you know when a dead-guy-risen, or a ghost, or whatever you think this risen Jesus is, is actually talking to you? You all seemed rather deflated when I then described what prayer is all about, and I think it is that simple. I think it sounded all quite normal to you, like prayer might just be talking and listening to Jesus, assuming of course he's alive again. (Why on earth would you attempt to pray/speak/listen to a dead guy?) This connection is certainly more than simply chanting the school prayer at assembly (although that does have its merits). But I think you probably intuitively know already that prayer is talking and listening to God. Then the bell went, regrettably. So we can finish this some other time.

Shalom, Mr Kemp.

Jack,

Hi again. Having declared in my first letter to you that outrageous claims will need substantive justification with evidence, I really only talked about one type of evidence, that of personal testimony, to justify the claim you balked at, that Jesus rose from the dead. (After all we all know that dead people are seriously dead and they don't come back to life, right?)

So, evidence. What about cultural context? I overheard Joe mutter on the day that Jesus probably wasn't actually dead. That is a common presumption. And Joe's response is actually demanded by our material worldview that we generally hold in the West. And

I'm glad he proposed this because we can now talk about how efficient the Romans were at crucifying people: we have to first establish that Jesus was dead. Seriously dead. The Romans were masters of the art of execution by crucifixion. Nailing someone to a cross was designed not only to maximize physical pain, but to impose personal, religious, and social shame as well (crucified naked, at eye level on a public and busy road, not way up there in the sky somewhere with a discretely placed loin cloth, the image enhanced by a beautiful sunset). Crucifixion was also designed to draw out the process of dying for as long as possible.

I don't need to go into the gruesome details. The observations that the four gospel writers make are adequate enough: Jesus up all night at a mock and illegal trial, 39 lashes, a crown of thorns, staggering with the cross (at least the cross beam) to Golgotha, stumbling numerous times, railway piton-like spikes hammered through his wrists and ankles, six hours hanging there naked in the blistering sun, then a spear thrust into his side. Witnesses watching all this. (Incidentally, the "blood and water" observation is medical evidence of death. Apparently the blood serum separates from the red blood cells on death. I'd have to revisit this with a conversation with a doctor.) Then being bandaged head to toe with 75 pounds (34 kilos) of spices and laid in a cold tomb with a huge stone rolled over its entrance and two Roman guards outside (at pain of crucifixion themselves if the tomb is tampered with). Jesus was seriously dead. If the resurrection didn't happen, and we conceded that people did see him after the crucifixion, then you have to say that after all this (and losing how much blood, and not having eaten or drunk for 24 hours), he revived in the tomb some how ("the coolness refreshed him" I hear you say), untangled himself from all that linen wrapping, folded it up neatly, rolled the massive stone away from the inside (no handles!), broke the Roman governor's seal (a capital crime), overcame two fully armed jumpy Roman soldiers and staggered off into the night naked. I don't think so. I'm a bit cynical about those claims.

I hope I didn't come across too preachy about this in class, but it does all sound a bit implausible. The cultural context really counts: the Romans knew what they were doing. Crosses dotted the countryside all across the Roman empire, particularly at the entrance to cities and on trade routes, to remind people who was in charge and what happens if you rebel.

So I wanted to add this cultural context to my first piece of evidence—my own testimony. Jesus was dead. Fully dead. Resurrection is an oxymoron if Jesus didn't die. (New word—oxymoron is a self contradiction.) If Jesus didn't die, and he managed to escape the tomb somehow, then, as a human, he would have later died normally. History has no record of this. (But that's not really an evidential claim, but an argument from silence.) But it does beg the question of why then a bunch of disciples—all the men and women who knew him in person and then all the thousands (yes, thousands—were they all hallucinating?) who then believed and became the church, would be willing to die themselves for a dead guy. The waves of persecutions of Christians that followed—empire wide and provincially too—didn't stifle or stunt this sudden new religious and social movement. I wouldn't be willing to die for a dead guy. Would you?

Shalom, Mr Kemp.

Olivia,

I've dropped two notes to Jack about that conversation we had in class about resurrection which you jumped into. I've suggested to Jack that a person's testimony—experience—does count as evidence. You asked a question about what Jesus said to me, and I responded by a short reflection on what prayer is all about. The second evidence is the cultural context of Jesus—particularly how efficiently Romans executed people—evidence that Jesus was seriously dead. Very dead. But also that these new Christians were so utterly convinced that he had risen as a new sort of spiritual being—a physical person who ate fish on the beach and walked on the road—that they simply could not deny it and refused to say "Caesar is Lord", but openly said "Jesus is Lord" from then on. Which cost them their lives.

ARE YOU ACTUALLY SERIOUS WHEN YOU CLAIM

What happened at Jesus' tomb on that first Easter Sunday morning is totally breathtaking. Breathtaking because it's all about the unexpected—classic Bible stuff. So much of the Bible plot is moved along by the most unlikely people, and in the case of the resurrection, it's women. Back at Easter time we read the whole story, and you'll remember that it's women who go to the tomb on Sunday morning and discover the tomb is empty (the two Roman guards had scarpered), and the tomb is standing wide open. Women had no legal rights back then so the whole story risks being written off as a fake because women are now the first to declare Jesus is risen. Who would believe women? That's why Peter and John then sprint to the tomb—doubters!!—and see it for themselves. This adds a note of authenticity, of factual sequence to the discovery. It's like Jesus riding into Jerusalem the week before on Palm Sunday on a donkey. A donkey! If you're going to be a king, you'd use an intimidating white stallion. And if you're going to rise from the dead, you'd have a multitude of angels and lightning and thunder and general overwhelmingness to announce it to the world, not three scared women.

Let me get ahead of you on this one. Other students over the years have said "ah, yes, sir, but how do we know the Bible is true—how do we know that these accounts of Jesus' resurrection are reliable"? There are four narrative accounts which come to us in the four gospels, and they're all a tad different. And that's good. If I asked four of you to write me a page on what happened on sports day, you'd all write something different, but you'd all be correct at the same time. Each account would be how you experienced sports day, and each would be valuable because of this. Each account would be just as authentic, true and reliable. So I think it is this type of detail—unexpected detail—of three unlikely grieving confused women that speaks of the gospels' authenticity here. And then later Thomas takes a week to catch up with the news. He doesn't doubt so much—he's got a bad rap for being "doubting Thomas"—but he is just a good 21st century scientist. He says "nah, I won't believe until I see the evidence". A top empiricist, no less. Why would the gospel accounts add in doubters, and mock their own questions, fears and disappointments? It seems that the writers of the story give us plenty of opportunity to question this resurrection event, but it nonetheless sticks. They are overcome by the evidence. Jesus himself keeps showing up. And it was first to the women.

So that's the gospels' accounts. Whether you can trust the overall nature of the Bible—that bigger question—we'll leave that for another day.

Shalom, Mr Kemp.

3

"Knowing stuff—how do you know what you claim is true?"

Olivia,

I think behind your question is a fundamental query about how do you know any of this stuff anyway? When we have that open question time in year 11 and you stick your questions all over the white board, it inevitably comes up. I've collected over 60 "how do you know" questions over the last five or so years. How do you know the Bible is true? How do you know Jesus rose from the dead? How do you know God created the universe? How do you know your Mum loves you? How do you know when politicians are lying? How do you know what heaven is like? Or how do you know Evolution is true? Or how do you know that this material world is all there is? I think these are essentially all the same question: how do we know, full stop.

What is knowledge? What is the process we go through to learn—to get to know—something? Is it possible to actually know anything for sure? What does certainty and proof then look like? Is knowing as a Christian different from knowing as a Buddhist, or an Atheist? And we could just keep piling on the questions. In the other half of my timetable at school, I teach *Theory of Knowledge* in the International Baccalaureate program—you know this, I think—and we wrestle with this question all the time. That's what that course is all about! And the question is fundamental to being human.

When we were talking about resurrection, we were also talking about some ways of knowing. Like what is the nature of evidence? Does my own personal experience count for anything? Can we rely on ancient historical texts to be true, to show us what actually happened? I claim I've experienced something because my senses inform me. I saw, tasted, touched, heard, smelled. Can you trust your senses? Also, knowing through testimony, trusting someone else's witness of something. They tell me something, or I read it or view it. (But that is always tagged to the testimony-giver's personal character: are they trustworthy and likely to be telling me the truth?) So much knowledge comes to us by testimony, from people we trust: teachers, editors, news-readers, doctors, authors, parents. So when it comes to knowing God—my experience of God counts for something. And other people's testimonies of their lives—their telling—also counts for something. When it comes to knowing if the Bible is true, we ask first if it is trustworthy, or rather, are the authors trustworthy, and if so, in what way? Does the Bible match what other historical sources say about history (like archaeology)? Is the Bible internally consistent? The Bible comments on itself: is it coherent? Does it make sense? The things that the Bible says are important, like the things we're supposed to do—well, do they work? Do they make us better people, if the Bible claims they should.

But we'd ask these questions of any text, I think. You ask it in English and History classes all the time. It's exactly the same question in History—can you trust the primary documents? And if so, in what way? In English, History and the Bible, you have to recognize genre. If love is the "[north] star to every wandering bark [i.e. ship]" (thanks, Shakespeare), then the lover in Song of Songs (the Bible) can speak of his beloved as "a mare among Pharaoh's chariot horses". (I'm not kidding: check it out in Song of Songs 1:9.) Love poetry behaves in certain ways, and when we understand this, then we can know what it's trying to say, and also what it's not saying. It's a question about how language works. The Bible uses metaphor a lot, along with other literary devices: it gives us ways to express perspectives about our experiences of ourselves, others, and God. These are just as true, and these claims hold just as much legitimate meaning as so-called scientific language. (More on this later.)

Agreeing together is also another way of knowing. To hear the endorsements of others who have looked at what you're looking at, or to get the "wait-a-minutes" from people you trust. Nevertheless, just because a gazillion people agree, doesn't mean they're right. (This is the Achilles' heel of Democracy I think.) But checking what you're committing to know with others is, well, a good check. In all the disciplines we study—English, History, Science, for example—we study the history of the discipline as well. The history of the knowledge method in each, the history of interpretation. It is really important for Christians too. How have other Christians interpreted the Bible and understood their Faith over the centuries? I need to check my knowledge—my spiritual knowing—with others around me today. Hence belonging in a community of knowing is important: this might be a cultural group or sub-group, or if you're a Christian, then it would include the church. To keep our knowledge and experiential claims accountable.

But I concede that knowing stuff is a bit of a leap of faith sometimes. People who claim to be non-religious (is anyone?) throw this leap-of-faith thing at Christians—like faith is an unjustifiable way of knowing anything. I don't buy that at all, especially from cynics. We all have faith that the other guy will stop at his red light. We first trust. Then understanding—head knowledge—follows. This sequence has been long debated in history. Does understanding come before faith? Or does faith come before understanding? I think the latter: we trust, have faith, put our confidence in ideas and people before we often understand what's really going on. Understanding follows and then kind of anchors our initial faith down. And once we know something, we then have the faith to expand on it and grow from it, trusting it to hold us. And it goes in a circle: faith and understanding talk to each other, build on each other, grow together. I can commit my heart to something or someone or a cause before I head-know that thing, person, or cause fully. I think we see this all the time in life. If everything was simply rational first—all brain/mind-understanding—then where does intuition, imagination and emotion come in? And love? To love is a bit of a leap of faith, I'd have thought.

Well I'm getting all philosophical now. That might not be a bad thing, because it's good to think this through carefully, no matter what age we are! Hope it makes sort-of sense.

Shalom, Mr Kemp

Olivia,

I sense you're not too convinced about all this knowing stuff in my previous letter. Yes, learning to live with paradox sometimes can be a challenge! Thanks for dropping that new word—paradox—into the conversation. And when we make extraordinary claims about the Bible—like it's historically trustworthy to tell us truth and even that it's the "word of God"—then I would also agree that we have to have some sort of way of establishing this. If you turn on your TV in the weekend, we have several Christian channels (why, I'm not sure—one would be more than enough), but if you pause and watch one of the preachers on TV for a while, you'll realize that there are different ways of handling the Bible. Some use it to proof-text ideas: they make a claim, and then find Bible texts to "prove" or justify that claim. Some use it really literally: "the Bible says so, so it must be true". Some read Bible texts like they're magic formulas. Others read into the Bible things that are quite illegitimate.

But I think the starting point is to recognize that the Bible is double-meaninged, or double-authored. It is a very human book, written and edited by ordinary people in real places and historical times, using the literary forms of their culture. So language and genre then become really important because they hold meaning. I'd say you have to read history as history, love poem as love poem, law as law, story as story, proverb as proverb, gospel as gospel, letter as letter, apocalyptic as apocalyptic (get your head around that genre—there's a challenge!). All these genres are in the Bible.

I think also it's really important to recognize language for what it is—a symbol system carrying meaning that we agree on. Let language be what it claims to be, and don't bend and bust the words, syntax, or grammar. Let literary forms behave according to their cultural rules: Hebrew poetry is very different to modern English poetry, for example. Its structure, rhythm and rhyme has to be learnt to recognize and appreciate it. In English narrative, the main idea of a paragraph is often at the beginning, and the climax of a story is towards the end. In Hebrew literature, you look for these in the middle.

Also we need to understand cultural practices and motifs and metaphors. A lot of this is not easily accessible because parts of the Bible were written thousands of years ago in ancient languages. That's why we have Bible scholars who spend decades learning the languages, and who dig up the Middle East and also spend a lifetime examining ancient scrolls in museums. I had to do Greek in my first theology degree so as to read the New Testament in its original language. My New Testament lecturer was an advocate: "so a preacher can't pull the wool over your eyes". But I discovered that knowing some Greek (and Hebrew for the Old Testament) really moors the translated English, and at the same time I observed that some of the Greek meaning is actually lost in translation, or muddied, or down right mistranslated!

What I've covered so far are two important notions: we ask the question first "what's behind the text"? Then we ask "what's inside the text?" Or, first, what's the context of the biblical passage we're reading, and then what's the content: what's it actually saying, and what's it not saying? For example, did you realize there are not three wise men in the Christmas story? (Don't let this year's Christmas cards deceive you!) Nor is there an apple in the garden in Genesis 3. There are three gifts in the Christmas story, and the fruit in the garden is, well simply, fruit. There's no apple at all. (I like to think Adam and Eve ate a mango or a papaya. Perhaps avocado?) When we have a closer more honest reading, then we start to see what's there, and then we start to know: we take the information, and turn it into knowledge when we embody it, take it on board, and start to read with our hearts and our heads. I think this is where knowledge is really at: knowledge is always relational. We relate to the text, and through the text we relate to the two authors (the human one and God!).

But then there's one more idea to note. When we've seen behind the text, and we've read inside the text, then we want to go beyond the text. (B.I.B—it's easy to remember!) Or context, content, then commitment (or courage to act). I like my alliteration! To know something is to apply it, let it change you in some way. Again, you allow this in English: ever tried to take some of Shakespeare's language and show off to a friend? I memorized his Sonnet 116 in school, just in case I needed it to woo a girl at some stage! And so why not allow this with the Bible (or any other religious literature)? If we're reading the Bible more honestly, using the framework of knowing I'm giving you, then you should hear the Bible "speak" to you, and hopefully move you to change. And because we say that God is the other author of the Bible (God influenced what the human writers were writing so that in effect they wrote adequately what God intended), then we can claim that God might be speaking to us through the Bible. And that, again, is quite a claim! But it's a small step of possibility that I embrace. That's why I read it every morning. Yeah, I know. The class was quite surprized when I said that I read the Bible every morning. Well I do because I want to know God and know how to live and know what's significant and know myself and know others. And then turn it into prayer and into action. I want to know God and be known by God. I have to first listen.

So that's a bit of a more Christian and biblical take on knowing. How do I know the Bible is true? We can really only answer that question when we handle it honestly and authentically, and I think the process I've outlined is a good starting place. If you want a fancy new word, it's called hermeneutics, the art of interpretation. Have you noticed that we use this process all the time? Think about getting off the bus this morning and arriving at school. You first establish the context of meeting your friends ("how was your bus trip into school? How was your soccer training last night?"—the past), then the content ("what's on your schedule today?"—the present) and then the commitment to act (now that we've understood where we're coming from and we're secure in re-establishing our friendship—I can trust you again—then "let's walk together to class"—application, now what?). Hermeneutics: the art of interpreting well. And that leads to knowledge. And knowledge is always relational.

Shalom, Mr Kemp.

Zac,

"Isn't all truth relative?" Thanks for asking that question. Your class mates agreed that this is a key question and when I pushed back we had quite a discussion! It seemed to everyone that it is a given that this is true. (Can you see the immediate oxymoron? But we'll get to that.) It may not matter at all what the elephant is standing on. You framed your question rhetorically: it's like a statement that you want me to agree with. But I resisted. We could tweak your question to open it up a bit: "is truth relative?" or flip it to "is truth absolute?", or more generally "what is the nature of truth" or what does it mean when we claim that "something is true", or "that's a true statement". Is the elephant standing on one thing that is solid? Is the elephant standing on truth? How far down does the elephant go before we find truth?

Just an aside, the Roman governor Pontius Pilate asked something close to this when he had the power to turn Jesus over for crucifixion: "what is truth?" or, in Latin, which he would have been speaking, *"quid est veritas"*. (Ever thought of screen printing a class T-shirt with this on it?) Granted, Pilate may not have been genuine in his question: he may have been exasperated at this point in events and used irony or sarcasm. Nevertheless, it was timely and to the point in that moment so long ago. This makes

How Far Down Does the Elephant Go?

it quite a famous question, one that we keep coming back to time and time again.

Plus it's a question that confronts us every day in this era of sordid global politics. Today there are claims to "alternative facts", where all big governing meta-narratives of story and ethics seem to have been sucked down the street drains and emptied into the sea. And tolerance has been elevated to such a virtue that we can have personal truths that we hold to—"my truth is different to your truth", or "let them live out their own truth", or "she's speaking her own truth". Everything is now relative, apparently, including truth, something now that you're contemplating with your question.

But I pushed back in class on logic alone. (And here comes the oxymoron.) When you make the truth claim that "everything is relative", that very statement itself is included in the "everything", making that statement relative, reducing it to sit along side every other truth claim. I suspect then it becomes meaningless. Why? Because there are some things that hold true, and hold true for all time, no matter what someone thinks about it. (This has, in the past, been simply called "fact".) Anyone who appeals to an absolute or all encompassing truth—a "fact"—risks being mocked or cancelled. So, let's talk about Alaska.

"Alaska exists" is an absolute truth claim. I have never been to Alaska, but I'm 100% confident it exists because of the evidence that supports that claim: every world map I've ever seen has Alaska on it. My friend who went there last year brought back evidence— actual artefacts—from Alaska. My friend is trustworthy in character. I have experienced his character to be truthful throughout our long years of friendship and I trust his testimony of his visit. He posted a selfie with the cop who gave him his speeding ticket in Anchorage. Plus Encyclopaedia Britannica has articles about Alaska, and that encyclopedia has proven over generations to be trustworthy and it is a universally accepted peer-reviewed source of reliable knowledge. To really justify my confidence in the truth claim that "Alaska exists" I could always go there myself to check it out. (Assuming of course I can trust my senses to give me accurate information of what I'd experience!) You can't say "I choose to deny

Alaska exists" or "I feel that Alaska might exist": it exists whether you believe it or not, and quite outside of what you feel about it. It's not a conspiracy. Something may well exist outside your experience of it. If you de-friend Alaska, it still exists. You can't cancel Alaska just because you don't like the cold or Sarah Palin.

Did you know that there are truth theories? It's a recognition that there are different types of truths. Most of how we speak each day is a poetic or phenomenological truth, often in metaphor. "You're a star!" And we also speak a lot using correspondence truth: what we claim as true corresponds to what is really happening. "You're reading this book". So we sense this second type of truth is accurate. I acknowledge I'm reading this book, and others can see I am too. The claim "I am reading this book" can be justified with acceptable evidence. (There are some issues with correspondence truth—come back to me and we'll keep talking about the problems of correspondence truth.)

Truth claims, of course, rely on language. We have to agree how language carries meaning, and language itself is culturally constructed. So when we make a truth claim, it has to be able to line up with—to be coherent and consistent with—other truth claims, using language. It has to make sense. It has to be consistent with the cultural network of beliefs it's made in. It has to "use" the language it's made in correctly, according to the accepted meanings, syntax, and grammar that gives it that very understandability. To make the truth claim that "there is a quabble shentle dinker there over", is not a coherent truth claim. "There is a black Labrador lying at my feet" is a coherent truth claim, as the claim makes sense in English, and it's a plausible event, and having a dog lying at your feet while sitting at a desk is a widely experienced phenomenon that readers will recognize (even though there is no-one in the house right now who could verify this claim). Again, there are some challenges to this type of truth: language keeps changing, and so meaning is never locked in to any word or sentence permanently. Language holds facts, inasmuch as language holds truth. So when someone claims to have "alternative facts" we smell a rat! There's an implicit oxymoron. We sense language is being manipulated: what the person means is there are alternative perspectives. And yet alternative facts, as a category of truth, are likely to be with us for a while!

There are other truth theories: pragmatic truth is about what works. "The bogey-man will get you if you walk out onto the street" is a truth claim. It's not ontologically true, but it does work if you tell that to your five year old niece, and it prevents her from running onto the street. ("Santa put the gifts under the tree" is a favorite, which we believe for a while, then grow out of it . . . or become Santa ourselves when we have kids to parent!) And consensus truth: it's what we all agree, truth by vote. (If we all agree that 2+2=5, then it does.) And relativistic truth, which is determined by context, by experience and culture. To say "there is a house at the end of the path" means something different to a Kalahari Bushman and an aristocratic English lady. Or contextual truth: "a spear is the best way to bring down a deer" is a truth claim that might hold for our Kalahari Bushman, but certainly not for a New Zealand farmer.

So there's quite a challenge I think to the question "how do you know if something is true?", and can we claim that "all truth is relative?" Maybe we can be more certain if a truth claim ticks off as many truth theories as possible at the same time. Maybe "pluralistic truth" works best, as something might be true in various ways: a claim is true if it is comprehensively so. "There is a house at the end of this forest path" is true in a number of ways: it corresponds to what actually is, it coheres and makes sense, it works and is useful, and we all agree the dwelling exists and it's there. I prefer the label "comprehensive truth" here, rather than "pluralistic truth", as that confuses us with the ideology of "pluralism", which again has to appeal to some sort of arbitrator of truth. If you have a number of truth claims lining up for your attention (pluralism), you need some sort of strategy to sort them, you'll need a commitment to a particular truth theory as a final judge.

I suspect you guys feel uncomfortable with truth statements that claim to be absolute. We often link them—illegitimately, I'd argue—to religion. "It's true because God says it is". Or "it's in the

Knowing stuff — how do you know

Bible so it must be true". This is, however, a legitimate theory of truth: sort of "truth claims from on high", whether as statements from God, or from religious literature, or from an authority like the United Nations Declaration of Human Rights. But deep down, I think we resist claims to absolute truth because it implies an authority over us, and we don't like that in this me-centered age we live in. My truth is mine because, well, it's mine. If an absolute truth claim has a claim on me, then I might be wrong and have to change!

However, I think we need to keep talking about truth. I sense we keep missing something, and I'm guessing that it might be that we keep thinking about truth as a proposition. Statements. Stand-alone de-contextualized claims. I suspect, however, that truth is more about narrative, about story, about overarching mythologies we all love. We wish to enter these, to be part of them, because they give us identity, belonging and a destiny. I want to enter into a true story, to participate in something that is true and is going somewhere. And I can't help myself here: Jesus moves beyond truth-as-proposition, because he himself claims to be Truth. He says "I am the Truth". In other words, truth is a person, not a proposition. And it's not just any person. It's Jesus himself. Wow! That's head exploding stuff. How can a person embody an abstract concept? But it's not foreign to you: we've met this idea in the personification of Wisdom. The film *The Shack* (2017)—remember we watched this in class—picks up on this idea: wisdom is a woman. And Papa says "Truth is a person, not a proposition": that in itself is quite a proposition! And I think we've already said that the Bible—all 66 books—forms one over-arching story. It claims to be a true story, with The Truth (a person) at the center of it, and the story invites everyone to join in and become an actor in the story, and see it out to the encore.

Shalom, Mr Kemp.

4

"Do you really think God actually created the world in seven literal days?"

Jamie,

I suspect the question in the box this morning about whether God created the world in seven actual days was yours. I'm guessing, but it is a question that keeps coming up amongst my students over the years. I make no apology for reading Genesis 1 and 2 in class, but I readily admit it can be head banging stuff, especially with a seemingly contradictory story going on in your science class, the evolutionary way of seeing our origins. And first we do have to say, I think, that evolutionary theory is also a creation story. I'm positioning this conversation now as a cultural one, not a scientific one (although we'll come back to that).

Actually, let's look at the scientific thing first. My first degree is in Zoology, which, looking back, is pretty much a degree in evolutionary theory as much as practical real-world discovery. Science is a way of knowing about the world around us—it's an empirical project. That's just a fancy way of saying science relies on our senses: we see, hear, touch the things and events we're examining; we bring order to our observations and experiences. Then we ask questions, form an hypothesis, set up tests to see if that observation is always the case. We then get others to check our work: I explained peer-review in class. Then we have to have our work published so it's useable (and testable) by others. It's a very rigorous way of learning about the world around us and it's been very powerful. In short, science asks three questions: can you observe it? can you measure it? can you repeat it? Simply put, these three questions drive the scientific project: it is a robust and rigorous way of discovery and prediction. If "yes" to those three questions, then truth emerges. And that truth holds and makes sense, until someone comes along and doubts it using new or different evidence. Science doesn't name absolute truths, but only poses conditional truths. When I was your age, the universe was 3.5 billion years old. Now it's 13.7 billion or so years old, I think. (The margin of error is 200 million years!) So did it age that number of billions of years in my short life span? No. Scientists have kept measuring it over and over again, looking at the evidence, devising more accurate instruments, testing different hypotheses.

So I think that when we get tangled up in conversations about the biblical creation story, we impose science on that conversation when we shouldn't. This is simply because we're so immersed in the scientific way of gaining knowledge and because the claim that God created in seven days is so, well, anti the gazillions of years needed for the evolutionary process to work out. But we shouldn't force science onto documents that don't claim to be scientific. Remember, the Genesis account—that's where the seven day creation is introduced in the Bible—were compiled probably about 2,500 years ago (and likely collated from even older stories, which were undoubtedly oral history of the Hebrews seriously ages ago), and science as we know it today—the scientific method—is only 400 or so years old, in its modern shape.

To get our heads into how Genesis and Science can talk to each other, we need to return to how language and truth claims work. Surprise, surprise. If you're sitting up Mt Eden in the center of Auckland city here and you and your girlfriend are having a romantic moment watching the sun go down over the Waitakere hills in the west, it's a moment to treasure and remember! The sky is all red and orange, and strong beams streak out through the dust and bounce off the clouds, and you say to your girlfriend "darling, what a beautiful sunset". (I don't know what terms of endearment your generation uses, but "darling" works here.) And all the school's senior rowers who are out on the Tamaki river at stupid-o'clock in the morning say "what a beautiful sunrise", as they sweat and heave and the coach yells at them from the support boat to stay focussed. But you and the rowers all know that the sun does not set (go down) or rise (come up)—the earth actually turns. You know this from your science classes. But you do not say to your girlfriend "darling, what a beautiful earth-turn". She'd think you're nuts. But that's technically—scientifically—what's actually happening. The earth is turning. But you see it as the sun setting or rising. This is a language and experience and perspective thing now, and it's true. The sun sets—it "goes down". But it's also true at the same time that the earth turns. Sun setting is phenomenological truth (you're experiencing a phenomenon from a point of view—the summit of Mt Eden, with your girlfriend), and "earth turning" is correspondence truth ("earth turn"—corresponds with what actually happens, the earth turns!). And both are true at the same time.

I'd suggest that the Bible tends to use phenomenological truth claims, that is, "sunrise-sunset" language, not "earth-turn" language. And I'd say that's the starting point in thinking about the creation accounts in Genesis 1 and 2. The text doesn't claim at all to be scientific in any sense. However, like all texts everywhere, it has a cultural context which is mediated to us by a certain genre. It's best read from within the cultural context it was written (which wasn't scientific). We need to read texts according to genre rules of that text.

Whew. Lots in this. I'll finish it later.

Shalom, Mr Kemp.

Jamie,

I had a bit of a chuckle when I learnt after that last letter that you are actually on the school rowing team. Were you out on the river at five a.m. this morning? So you do know all about sunrises and the potential to acknowledge that sunrise-sunset language could be an appropriate way of keeping ancient texts in context. Great connection.

So if we are free from having to see Genesis through the lens of science, then all sorts of possibilities open up. First, Genesis 1 and 2 is not the only place in the Bible where creation is talked about. The Psalms (poetry and songs) and some of the prophets and in the New Testament too there are passages that are clearly creation passages. So it's good to be reminded that the Bible talks about itself, or interprets itself and comments on itself. Not surprising really as it was written or compiled over about a 600 year period, and latter authors may well have had copies of the older texts in front of them as they themselves were writing! What I'm saying is that to consider the Bible's claims about creation, you have to look at what the whole Bible says about creation, not just the first two chapters of Genesis. Remember, hermeneutics is the art of interpretation, and the first task is to examine context, what's behind the text.

Plus the biblical texts use standard literary strategies of ancient literature (you know about these from English class): you can even feel the ancient rhythm and rhyme coming through in the English, particularly in Genesis 1. It feels like the reader is chanting. Plus there are mnemonic devises (stuff to help you remember), like patterns of significant numbers. If you remember the Exodus story—where Moses is leading the people out of slavery in Egypt—you could well imagine the people sitting around their campfires at night chanting and singing Genesis 1. This God who created the world, is now creating us as a people! I'm speculating, but it certainly is plausible. (Just an aside: even if the genre of Genesis 1 is something like camp-fire song or narrative poetry or something similar, it doesn't mean it isn't true. Robbie Burns' profound claim that "love is like a red, red rose" is poetry, and it's true!). A claim does not have to be literal to be true.

So if we allow a cultural lens rather than a scientific lens to read the creation stories, then I think this genre and contextual

How Far Down Does the Elephant Go?

strategy will yield more to us. Where were these texts first located and how do the texts work? I'm saying that language is really important and how the Hebrews wrote also must count for something. For example—and this becomes really important—the number 7 is widely recognized as a symbol representing perfection, order, completeness, and beauty. There is some numerology happening in Hebrew culture. (I wouldn't want to lose myself in it, but it is there.) And you can probably see where I'm going with this now. We can see that using 7 might be a way of adding to the phrase "and it was good" at the end of the creation of each day to endorse that God's creative acts were perfect, orderly, complete, beautiful, and most importantly fit for purpose, doing what God intended. We read in the first chapter of Exodus that Moses as a baby was a "fine" baby. This is the same word as "good" in Genesis 1. So I'm thinking quality, potential, usable for God's purposes, fit for purpose. Creation and Moses. Both significant beginnings! And also, remembering that the Hebrews were ex-slaves escaping 430 odd years of bondage in Egypt (escaping under Moses' leadership), they seriously want to separate themselves from the gods of Egypt and learn about this new God—YHWH (pronounced something like "Yahweh"; incidentally the same God as the God of their forefathers)—who claims to be the only true God. If you read Genesis 1 and 2 as an argument against the Egyptian gods (in fact, all of the Ancient Near Eastern gods), then again we're reading this in sunrise-sunset language, not earth-turn language. And it's just as true: one God, not many; a covenantal, loving God, not a vindictive merit-demanding god of the Egyptians or Babylonians.

So coming back to the question in the box (was it yours?), I'd concede that some Christians hold on really tightly to a literal seven days of creation. As a scientist myself, I'd have to acknowledge the good work that my colleagues do and recognize the truckload of evidence for an old universe, for evolutionary change that is evident and the likes. But as a Christian, I recognize in the Genesis accounts of creation that this God—YHWH—is unique (contra the Egyptian gods), introduces himself to his people the Hebrews in cultural ways they recognize and understand (the God who created the universe continues to create people and nations), and affirms that the universe is fit for purpose—it's "good".

One last thought: the ancient Hebrews reading these creation texts wouldn't have thought of any other means of creation, that there wasn't a god creating. Of course God creates the world. That was their worldview, that's what their elephant was standing on. All the ancient literature demonstrates that everyone believed that 3,000 years ago! The question of "how did God create?" would not have been of any concern to them. That's a 21st century concern. That God created is what was important. We need to let the texts—both ancient and scientific—speak for themselves, from within the contexts of those texts.

We alluded to much of this in class, but it's been good to try and outline this now in writing. Hope it's starting to make sense?

Shalom, Mr Kemp.

Jamie,

Just one more thought on this creation stuff, and the conversations with Science (particularly re Evolution). Hopefully you're picking up that I'm a bit slow to jump into conversations that at first look simply black and white. There is always nuance, and I think it's often best to say "wait a minute: where's this question coming from?" and "what initial work do we have to do to recognize bias, assumptions, definitions, and worldview? How far down does this elephant go? We need to clear the ground of the cultural and linguistic rubble before we can actually address the question.

Like I've been suggesting with the metaphor of the elephant, often it comes down to our own assumptions first, and then also genre. This is the sunset-earthturn thing again. I think you guys in class often dump a whole bunch of bias and cliché into the conversations without first examining where you're coming from. I catch myself doing it too. I forget to examine what the elephant is standing on. I'd say first to treat ancient literature as ancient literature (not scientific document) and treat science as science (not ancient historical literature). Genre rules apply. And each genre must be consistent with its own rules: a scientist should never say anything about the beginning of the universe. (Wha.? I hear you say). Yes, we scientists say stuff about the beginning of the universe all the time, but we shouldn't. For the simple reason that the beginning is not observable, not measurable and not repeatable. That is simplistic, I concede, but it's within scientific methodology boundaries, nonetheless. Science can say a lot about the time immediately after the beginning of the universe, but it certainly can't answer the question why there is something (the universe!) and not nothing, that is, say anything about the original cause. Science loves models and prediction: scientists will create models of how the universe began, based on data about how it is now and with assumptions that we think are justifiable today, but we have to recognize these models are only conjectures, not facts. They are often very good models and models that "work" and are helpful for when we need them. But the models keep changing. Scientific knowledge is never set in stone. All honest scientists will acknowledge this.

Likewise ancient texts—or historians or theologians who handle ancient texts—don't (or shouldn't) say anything about science (or the scientific method). You can think of ancient texts being primarily about relationships: with one-self, with each other, with the gods, with the world. There are claims in ancient texts that look scientific (for that's what science is first of all, human observation of the world around us), but these "scientific" claims within the texts are not there because of a scientific method of enquiry. Ancient Hebrews knew scientific stuff—they observed the world around them and identified the patterns in it: the water cycle, the limits of tides, the behaviors and life cycles of animals are some examples. But they understood these things as part of a world that was "good", that is, created fit for purpose by the one God, YHWH.

Probably enough for now. Plenty here to chew on. Let's keep the conversation going. I'll see where the rest of the class want to take this next week.

Shalom, Mr Kemp.

5

"If God is so good, then why is there evil in the world?"

Johnny,

You dropped THE question into class yesterday. THE question. Maybe it's the question that I think everyone should be asking. "If God is good, then why is there evil in the world?" Or sometimes it's "why is there suffering in the world"? (This second form of the question equates suffering with evil, which it may or may not be—bookmark that for another time.) So for now, let's just go with your question as you asked it using "evil" as the key problem. I'm surprised that more students don't ask it.

I have discovered over the years that when students latch onto a key question, it often has a personal context, and when this particular question pops up—with a bit of a prod from me—I'm not surprised if there is a current tragedy or problem that has prompted it. Maybe you have something going on that provoked this question? And it is a very, very important question: we are deeply outraged that because God must be good (by definition), there is an incongruence with what we see in the world—there's a lot of evil around, often in the form of violence. And heaps of suffering. We interpret this as incompatible with our understanding of the nature of God.

Just to be fancy, the question you asked is the question of theodicy, and humans have been debating this for as long as humans have been on the planet. We assume, presume, hope that God is good. We want God to be good. Morally good. If we're talking about the Christian God, then we are told that indeed this God reveals himself as good. I'm pleased—as an aside—that you assume of course that God actually exists. The question then is not about the existence of God, but about the moral character of God, or the will or desire of God to act. We assume that if God is good then God is somehow responsible for the suffering and evil in the world. It's an affront to God and us that there is suffering and evil. God should just get rid of it all. Another student was more forthright: "why doesn't God just get rid of all the shit in the world?" This presumes that God is able to and willing to get "rid of the shit in the world": that God has the power to remove it, and that God has the desire to do so also.

I agree with the sentiment. But I also want to pause here. Your question presumes a certain type of evil, and it presumes a certain type of solution, namely, we want God to act now, immediately, to take evil completely away. Get rid of it. And we presume a certain type of god, that God will jump to do what we want. We readily expect God to work according to our agenda, to be in our image. I suspect it's often a question coming out of deep personal pain, or out of a crisis that the questioner is experiencing. Maybe for you? Maybe not. In other words, life is tough, life sucks, and God should do something about this. Or if I'm brutally honest, I'm blaming God for the crap in my life when it's not particularly God's fault, but probably more to do with my own stupidity and bad choices. We're trying to pass the buck to God. Again, maybe, maybe not. But we sort of intuitively sense that the world isn't the way it should be. And that God must be responsible for it. It seems obvious that because there is evil, well, God therefore doesn't exist, or doesn't care.

If God is so good, then why is there evil

Did you hear my pushback in class? Maybe God has taken evil away, or started to take evil away, maybe in a different time frame, and it looks different to what we expect? That's possible, but it's outside what we want. (Why would God necessarily have to work to my or your schedule?) Or maybe God has promised to take evil away in the future (and left us some sort of deposit or guarantee of that), but is allowing evil to continue for now for reasons that are a bit beyond us. All of these are possible, but we tend not to jump into those because we want evil to disappear now, today, out of my life: we want an evil-free, suffering-free life on our own terms, now, immediately. And again, we need to be brutally honest with ourselves here: by "evil" do we really mean "those things that merely inconvenience me"? Like "damn, I missed the cut on the football team again" or "why can't the supermarket ever have my favourite chocolate". Or, alternatively is evil simply the opposite qualities of God, sort of like The Force in the Star Wars stories, dark and light. Or does evil have agency: is it embodied in institutions, persons, systems, and it's dark, sinister, bad, destructive, violent, inhumane, degrading?

I start my Year 13 classes each year with an exercise where we admit by the end of our first period—after quite some debate—that there is both good and evil in the world at the same time. This year my students called it "beauty and ugliness", which I liked, and it works. All my three Year 13 classes conceded we live in a tension between this beauty and ugliness: the world is awesome and it's good to be alive (but life can really, really suck as well); there is a huge amount of brutality, injustice and downright brokenness around, but amongst all that, there is gold, new shoots, and caterpillars-turning-into-butterflies.

The book of Job in the Old Testament probes this question of theodicy. It's a fascinating book, despite being a bit of a mind-bender to read. But what is obvious by the time you get to the end of it is that God will work out God's own agenda according to God's own time, not according to our expectations, and basically "shut up and sit down young man. Who are you to question God?" Which is a bit of a tough response and a brutal conclusion, but it does remind me that this was the problem in Genesis 3, where Adam and Eve thought they could run the world better than God, then screwed it all up. I'm sure that if I was running the world, there would be a whole lot more evil in it.

Can I suggest that a starting point to living with theodicy is the affirmation that God is good, and God is just, even though we see evil around us. It's a problem about the evil we experience, not the nature of God. And, like in the film *The Shack*, God challenges Mac with that very question: "you don't trust me that I'm good". I remember being challenged by that when we watched the film earlier in the year. It sounds a tad trite, but it is a trust statement. It's like a foundation: you've got to build on some faith commitment first, and then understanding follows. Anyway. Great conversation so far. I hope this resonates with you?

Shalom, Mr Kemp.

Kate,

Johnny told me he'd talked with you about my response to his question "if God is good why is there evil in the world?" Great to see you guys continuing to wrestle with this outside of class! I totally get it though when you challenge me when I might claim "God is good and God is just", and yet we look at the news feed in the morning, and there is war in Ukraine, starving millions in Sudan, and lying politicians everywhere. Obviously God hasn't cleaned up the place yet! How do we live in this tension of "beauty and ugly" at the same time—those were the words my Year 13 classes used.

I think it does come back to the resurrection of Jesus, but I have to introduce you to a new idea—that's the Kingdom of God. The resurrection of Jesus and the Kingdom of God are intimately connected. You can think of the resurrection as the starting gun going off for Kingdom of God stuff.

Kingdoms aren't too common today, or popular. They seem a bit old fashioned. We've moved to republics and democracies (or dictatorships, which I suppose could be considered really bad kingdoms). The coronation of King Charles III was fascinating, spectacular and rooted in ancient traditions, but we all know that King Charles III is more about symbol than power. But let's roll with the idea for now.

If you read any of the four gospels (Matthew, Mark, Luke or John), you'll see that Jesus talked about the "Kingdom of God" a lot. Like, really a lot. (In Matthew, he talks about the Kingdom of Heaven, but same same, different audience.) Here he's not talking about a piece of land: it's not like the United Kingdom of Great Britain which is clearly defined as an island with a big ocean around it. Actually, "kingdom" in the New Testament Greek is the same word as "empire"—and the Roman empire had clear borders. Think of the Goths on the northern border always hassling the Romans. (Remember the opening scene in the film *Gladiator*?) Jesus uses the word kingdom more like "reign" or "rule" or "influence". We use it like this in English too: the "kingdom of Bill Gates" might refer to the influence of Bill Gates through his company Microsoft or through his philanthropy. Or the "kingdom of Rupert Murdoch" is the influence he has through all the media companies he owns. Jesus uses the expression like that: "the Kingdom of God is among you" or "when the Kingdom of God comes" and the likes. He's talking about the influence, the rule, the reign of God amongst people. If he implies territory, then it is the whole earth, much bigger than the ancient borders of the land of ancient Israel.

So this idea of Kingdom of God might be where an answer to Jamie's question of theodicy could lie. God is working on evil to another agenda that we often can't appreciate (we want evil done with now!). God has started to work on evil through the life, death and resurrection of Jesus. We celebrate this at Easter. This is where the Kingdom of God really kicks off. The crucifixion of Jesus is huge here: the cross is like a lightning rod which discharges a thunderous attack of evil and earths it immediately. And just to prove it counted for something, Jesus rises from the dead on the third day after. The very nature of the universe has changed—God's reign, rule, influence is in a new phase. But that's not an end: it's the end of a beginning. (You can see Kingdom stuff foreshadowed in the Old Testament too.) The Easter event is Part I of a two-part event.

Jesus said he's coming back, and the writers of the New Testament certainly expect this. This is where the tension between beauty and ugly—goodness and evil, justice and corruption, peace and violence—lies. It explains that God has started to clean the mess up, but it's a process that's not finished yet. That finish will come at Jesus' second coming. I've got a great illustration for this, and I'll share it with you when I write again.

Shalom, Mr Kemp.

Kate,

So I said I'd try and illustrate this Kingdom of God idea, when I signed off my previous letter. And yes I am saying that the New Testament claims we're living in a sort of in-between time, between a first coming of Jesus (that's where we date our calendar from, and why we celebrate Easter), and a second coming of Jesus, which hasn't happened yet.

I've picked up this illustration from way, way back somewhere. A professor called George Ladd came up with it in the late 1950s. But it works. It's a WWII picture. To understand how WWII ended in Europe, you need to know two dates: D-Day, 6th June, 1944; and V-E Day (Victory in Europe day), 7th May 1945. Notice there is exactly 11 months between them. When did the end of the war occur? Well, it was a two stage ending. The Allies had come to the conclusion that you had to "put boots on the ground"—wars are won by real soldiers on the ground: you can't just keep on bombing the enemy from the air.

D-Day was the date where all the combined forces of Britain, Canada, and the US (with some help from us down-under in New Zealand and Australia!), landed at the beaches of Normandy, France. There was an horrific tally in lost lives—the beaches had to be totally secured and the German forces defending them had to be completely overcome. The horror of the challenge is captured in films like *Saving Private Ryan*. The Allies did manage to do this eventually, and the supply chains were set up, the Allies hunkered down: they had their first toe-hold in Europe itself. It was like giving notice to Hitler: "we're here! We're on our way. Look out!". If we change the metaphor, it was like a bank deposit: here's the first bit, and more's coming. In some sense you could say that as soon as the beaches in Normandy were secured by the Allies, the end of the War was guaranteed. It obviously wasn't finished, but its conclusion was inevitable.

And then for 11 months, these Allied forces still had to make their way across France, to deal finally with Nazi Germany. They had to literally walk and drive from Normandy to Berlin, taking back Europe house by house, village by village, bridge by bridge: a sort of grand mopping up, flushing out every single German brigade or isolated soldier, checking inside every barn, looking under every bridge, examining every hedge. When they finally got to Berlin and the Nazis surrendered, only then was the War really over—"Victory in Europe"—and the whole of the continent burst out in dancing, street parties, hugging, crying, and, more importantly a peace. A real peace. Not just the absence of the violence, but the building of something new: not just re-building Europe, but imagining a new kind of Europe.

So coming back to this two-stage Jesus event: the first coming of Jesus is like D-Day. The sacrifice through death (the soldiers dying on the beaches) guarantees the victory, an ultimate future victory. The second coming of Jesus is like V-E day, the final bursting forth of celebration when all that evil will finally be done away with. The intermediate time—the 11 months between D and VE days—is the current time we live in. We live in this big mop up stage. Goodness is conquering evil person by person, family by family, village by village, until that day when at Jesus' second coming we can then say the Kingdom of God is here fully. In fact, the Bible talks about this as the creation of "a new heaven and a new earth" (not just Europe, in our example). Not just returning to Eden, but envisaging something completely new.

I've always found this illustration really helpful, because it explains some things. It explains why, even though we claim God is good, there is still evil around (remember theodicy?) It explains why we live in a tension of both good and bad at the same time (beauty and ugly). It explains prayer: some prayers are answered and some are not (we are in an in-between time). It gives us hope: we know that the battles will be won eventually, even though life sucks today. I know that death (my death, and everyone else's) isn't the end: a new heaven and a new earth are coming, and Jesus' resurrection guarantees everyone else's.

Well that was quite a headful. Hope it was helpful. Let me know if you want to kick this around a bit more.

Shalom, Mr Kemp.

6

"What is the right thing to do, and why should I do it?"

Will,

How do you know to do the right thing? How do you know what the right thing is to do? That's a great question, and it falls in the general category of ethics. Ethics is about knowing how to live, what decisions should I make here, now, and why. In fact, every time we see the word "should", it is probably an ethics question. Why should I stop at a red light? Why should I pay for that chocolate bar? Whom should I marry? It does require some intentional engagement, and each of us forms ethical boundaries over a life time, I'm discovering. More obviously, ethical boundaries are imposed on us. These are the laws, rules, codes of behavior we have to comply with and fit into our lives. We have this implicit agreement—a "social contract"—that we're all going to get along and we need some standards that we all agree on so as to simply live well together without sliding into social chaos. When I go through a green light, I'm assuming the guy going the other way will stop at his red light. I'm trusting that the other driver will hold up his

How Far Down Does the Elephant Go?

end of the social contract. The carnage created if he doesn't is good reason enough to think that ethics might be really important!

This is why we're spending so much time on Moses' "10 Words" in class. You might have first heard of them as The 10 Commandments. You find them in two places in the Bible: Exodus 20 and Deuteronomy 5, but they're implied everywhere. I'd claim that they are fundamental to the very foundation of our Western civilization—all our laws, rules, workplace ethics codes and the likes I reckon can be traced back to these commands. In the past, we've spent all of Year 13 just looking at these commandments, and there is heaps in them to explore.

I don't want to overload you, so will unpack just one idea here. And I think it's foundational to how we think about ethics—how we live, how we make decisions, and how do you know what the "right thing" to do is. The second half of Moses' list is five "do nots": do not murder, do not commit adultery, do not steal, do not bear false witness/lie, and do not covet. They're negatives, and at first read, you might think that Christianity is just a killjoy by telling us what not to do. But let's open this up a bit through a study of some children in a playground. In 2006, The American Society of Landscape Architects did some research in order to design a playground for a new orphanage in the US state of Alabama. It went something like what follows (and you can check it out at asla.org website):

They set up a study of children playing. The architects took a group of children to a standard playground with normal playground equipment: swings, slides, sand-pit, see-saw and the likes, like the ones you find in any park in the city, but it didn't have a fence around it. Then they said "go and enjoy", and they recorded where each child was, say, every 20 seconds. They observed that all the kids played on or really closely to the playground: on the equipment, not running more than a meter or two from the playground, even though there were no boundaries, and they could have run off. But nobody did!

Then the architects took the same group of children to another playground with a fence right around it. Everything else was

What is the Right Thing to Do, and Why

exactly the same. They recorded where each child was at any one time, and they discovered that the children now used the whole play area, across the field right up to the fence: they initiated wide games like tag, bull-rush, football. They played on both the playground equipment and all over the field, right up to the fence.

The experimenters interpreted this in terms of perceived freedom and creativity. On the second trial, when a fence was imposed—a "do not go past here" barrier—the kids felt safer, and so they played more widely. In other words, even though a barrier had been erected, their freedom had increased. For the first trial, the kids kept in close to the playground because they felt insecure, not knowing where the boundaries were. Even though they had enormous freedom of place to go anywhere they pleased, they didn't: they had lost their actual freedom, and clustered together to create a security that they perceived hadn't been given to them. Amazing.

So I'd put it to you that the rules we live by (stop at a red traffic light) actually create freedoms. (You get across the intersection safely and stay alive!) Same with Moses' last five commandments. If you now flip them around, you can think of some possible positives: do not murder (that's the fence) becomes "promote and celebrate life in all its joys" (inside the fence). Do not commit adultery (the fence) becomes "enjoy great sex with your one spouse" (inside the fence). Do not steal (the fence) becomes "enjoy your work and all that is materially good in this world that is yours" (inside the fence). Do not bear false witness/lie (the fence) becomes "celebrate truth". In fact Jesus had something to say here: "the truth will set you free"! And then the last one is confronting: do not covet (the fence) becomes "enjoy everything that comes to you as a gift, and be content with that" (or something similar). The trouble with this last one is that our whole society is built on coveting. Advertising is the fuel for this. This might be quite a challenge: it is a personal discipline to train yourself to be satisfied with the good gifts that come your way. At least, I find this.

One last thought. The trouble with us humans is that if there is a fence, we like to know what's on the other side. In fact we usually climb it, or break it down. If we're forbidden something, we usually break the rule, just because we can. "What right do you have to constrain my free choice?" we question. The fence is put there to demarcate ownership (perhaps the playground belongs to God?) and where safety is (inside) and danger is (outside). What if that playground was next to a river or a freeway? Climb the fence and you risk drowning or being taken out by a truck. The fence is there for a reason.

So if you imagine yourself into this study of the children, then the "do-nots" can become quite attractive! The great thing about the 10 Words of Moses (the 10 Commandments) is that they start with God introducing himself: "I am the Lord God who brought you out of Egypt, out of slavery." God has initiated a rescue, a saving, an act of grace before he tells us how to live. So ethics? How do we live? What decisions do we make? The playground and the field may actually belong to God—they are places of grace that God has given us. The fence too is a gift. When and where we play inside the fence is really up to us: I don't think God really cares whether you play on the slide, in the sand pit, or football out on the field. All of life inside the fence is to be enjoyed. You choose. And God celebrates this, surely?

Let me know what you think. Is this a good way to frame ethics? You may well come back with the question "why should I follow this particular code of ethics"? Or indeed, any code at all. Love to keep talking with you about it. And I fully admit that when we reference ourselves to codes of ethics (God given or otherwise!), well they feel at first read quite restrictive. But one other thing: you told me you had read Jesus' Sermon on the Mount in Matthew 5–7. Do you think there could be any overlap with Moses' commandments? Does Jesus cancel, modify, endorse, expand, fulfil Moses commands? Maybe all of these? Thoughts?

Shalom, Mr Kemp.

Tom,

Well that was an interesting class. You guys in Year 13 inevitably come up with that sex question at some stage each year. I do work

WHAT IS THE RIGHT THING TO DO, AND WHY

hard at creating safe spaces for these conversations. It's a really important question, and one that no doubt is front and center for you as you're all thinking about the immediate future and relationships and identity, and well, pretty much everything is related to it. I'm glad you felt comfortable and safe enough to talk together.

So, your question: "is sex before marriage OK?". When we do the open box activity, there are usually about five variations of this question for every twenty or so questions in the box. It's obviously on your minds—it's usually a guy who owns up to putting the question in the box. But I've noticed the girls pay attention too!

As you know I always recommend pushing the question around a bit to find context. Where is the question coming from, what's behind it, who's asking it, what are the consequences of how we answer? In other words, the elephant again. On good evidence over many years, I suggest that the question is usually asked for either of two reasons. Firstly the student has already, or is contemplating having sex and wants to justify him/herself. Secondly, 17 year olds are trying me out, and particularly because you have these ideas about what a Christian response is. Obviously "No" is the Christian response, right? Well, maybe. But this answer is simplistic, and like I always recommend, there is more nuance. And even if we conclude "no", then we still have to know why. It's like there's a perception out there that Christians like to kill all the good fun—no this, no that, no sex before marriage. Killjoys! (But maybe it's a fence thing—maybe there is more freedom when there is a fence?) Before there's a definitive yes or no from me (and why), let's clear some ground: what is the sex we're talking about, and what is marriage (and what is Christian marriage, particularly)?

First, sex. Behind the question I reckon is the real question of "how far can we go before it is wrong"? It's like "where is the line over which it is a sin" (to use a very Christian word). Or "how much fun can we have before there's a real problem or price to pay, like wrecking someone's life? How much petting can I get away with?" The media and our movies don't particularly help us here as full-on sex is seen as normal, like everyone does it on the first date. Well I've been around a bit, and sex on the first date is not that common, and I reckon there is a lot less sex happening than the movies would have us believe (and actual surveys endorse this, if, of course, people respond honestly on surveys about their sex life!). Sexual acts are not inevitable in good relationships. But we'll come back to that soon. (And as an interesting aside, there is sex in the Bible—both good sex and really bad sex, like gang rape).

And marriage. Before you can answer the question, we have to unpack what marriage actually is. Here the Bible has something to say—it is the leaving of the growing-up family you're in, and cleaving (binding) to your partner. It's a one on one thing: man with woman, woman with man. But apart from that, the Bible leaves plenty of cultural space open for interpretation. Wedding ceremonies in ancient Israel were really different to wedding ceremonies today. The Bible strongly implies that marriage is God's idea—in some sense, marriage is a three way relationship: man, woman and God. And then this three-way relationship is endorsed by some authority, usually the State, or at least some sort of civil agreement between the two families of origin.

I learnt while I was engaged that I would be marrying a whole family. Get used to that idea. Plus we recognized that we had to sort out things like how we communicate, how were we going to manage our finances, how we'd shape and discipline children. Who and when each would work or be at home, how to build family routines and memories, and also to continue to be best of friends (for that is how the relationship starts, hopefully). Much of this is often mundane and some times hard work. Most importantly I think—and the Bible again implies this—you need to be together in vision: what are your life goals and aspirations and sense of meaning and purpose? If you're going to give up your singleness, then how are you as a together-partnership going to be better than the mere sum of each of you?

At this point, I recall a brilliant illustration that one of your peers gave one year. Yes, a year 13 student piped up in class with this illustration. Remember, this is yours—one of your generation's pictures.

"Sir" he said. "Marriage is like a cake. All those things you said—friendship, memories, good times, compatibility, communication—you can have all of that in solid and growing friendship—with anyone and everyone. Plain old uncomplicated friendship. You mix those all together in a big mixing bowl, and you can bake it and you can have an excellent cake, excellent friendships".

He went on. "Sex is the icing".

"How do you mean?" I asked.

"Well, the icing goes onto the cake: you have to make the cake first. You put the icing on at the end, after the cake is well baked. So your friendship, and then your engagement—that's all about finding the ingredients, mixing them in well, getting them in their right proportions, and then baking the mix. And a cake is a good cake if it's put together by following the recipe—the rules. And you can't put icing on the cake immediately after taking it out of the oven. The cake has to cool down. The cake has to be ready for the icing. It all goes horribly wrong otherwise."

And then he said something which I think is quite countercultural: "In fact, you don't really need icing for a great cake. You can have a great cake without icing: we never have icing on our Christmas cake at home each year. So, likewise, you can have great friendships without sex. If your friendships are well mixed and baked and have followed the recipe, then the icing seems rather over-rated. Besides, you can't add the cake to the icing. You can't have the sex, then build the relationship."

And then he landed his reflection with a comment I'll never forget: "you can have an excellent cake without icing: excellent relationships, without sex. But if you eat only icing without the cake—you'll make yourself really, really sick".

And that, I think, is a great answer to your question.

Shalom, Mr Kemp.

Kay,

I agree with you that this whole AI thing is really relevant. It's definitely in the field of Ethics. Should we or should we not use

AI at school? And if so, for what activities? You asked "what's the relevance of the Turing Test?" and that's a great question because it seeks to evaluate how human a computer might become! You'll want to know exactly what the Turing Test is, so as to make the most of that poster I've got you designing to answer one of those five questions. So, essentially you're asking when will a computer genuinely demonstrate sentience? Are we actually there yet? And if/when they do, will that be a threat to us or an opportunity? The whole AI thing is quite a challenge isn't it? Should we be creating intelligent computers? And how would we recognize an intelligent computer: what would it have to do for us to know this? We're all quite alarmed because of what the movies have come up with already—*The Matrix,* for example—demonstrating what might happen if our computers get a mind of their own! Bye bye humanity.

The test was devised by Alan Turing, the WWII code breaker, in 1950. The 2014 film *The Imitation Game* showed us something of his life and achievements. What a genius! The test seeks to establish if a computer can exhibit intelligent behavior which is equivalent to human behavior, or at least indistinguishable from it. A computer and a human do the same tasks and if a third party human simply can't distinguish any difference in the results, then we'd say the Turing Test has succeeded. Something of this is starting to appear in the recent availability of AI generated text through ChatGPT (and other programs and apps) which a few of you have discovered. In some sense we're there already—I've put up some ChatGPT generated texts in front of you already, without telling you and you've not noticed any difference whatsoever! I've fed questions to ChatGPT and it has collated answers for me that look like a human has generated them. Was I wrong to do this?

So to the movie then that we've jumped in and out of: *Ex Machina* (2014). I'm loving listening into your group discussions as you work on your posters. Nathan, you'll remember, is the main AI creator and programmer; Ava is the humanoid robot he's created (and very sensual robot to boot—she's not an android, but a gynoid); and Caleb is the one who is used in the film to test Ava's ability to be sentient and humanlike. (Nathan asks Caleb at one

WHAT IS THE RIGHT THING TO DO, AND WHY

point: "do you think Ava likes you?") These types of films have been around for a while though: the biggest question is "can we build a computer that will actually demonstrate love"? Maybe, maybe not. But not only "can": should we build a computer that demonstrates love? Perhaps the ultimate Turing Test? Here again are the questions you're working with: each group has one and I'm looking forward to seeing your finished posters:

1. Do you think Nathan is morally justified in creating Ava (the gynoid). Why? Why not?

2. *Ex Machina* raises questions about the ethics of creating AI that can mimic or surpass human intelligence. What are the potential risks and benefits of developing AI to that level?

3. The Turing Test assumes that intelligence is primarily demonstrated through language and conversation. Do you think this is a fair assumption, or are there other forms of intelligence that should be considered when evaluating AI systems?

4. In *Ex Machina*, what ethical concerns arise when AI entities like Ava gain knowledge about human emotions and vulnerabilities and how do they utilize that knowledge?

5. How does *Ex Machina* challenge traditional notions of knowledge and consciousness by blurring the lines between human and machine, and what ethical dilemmas does this raise regarding the nature of knowledge itself?

I'm not going to tell you the end of the film. You'll have to watch the whole thing at home in your own time. Easy enough to find in the IMDB website.

The words *ex machina* are an abbreviation of the longer phrase *deus ex machina*, which means "god from the machine". It was a theatrical device used in ancient Greek plays to bring in God (an actor swung in by ropes) onto the stage to free up some plot dead-end that needed the intervention of God to sort it out. So it's come to mean something like when a person or solution is suddenly introduced into a problem without notice or warning and offers a contrived or fantastical solution to an insoluble problem. (I got that from Wikipedia!) So, great name for a movie, right? And I find the end quite alarming. Ava passes the Turing Test and the consequences are.... well I won't tell you. But is she still out there living amongst us? How would you know?

However, I think behind the film is the question: "what does it mean to be human?" This might be the fundamental question, and we don't know how far down this elephant goes! If we can now create robots that pass the Turing Test, does that make them human, or does that compromise our humanity in some way? It's a fundamental question about identity. In what ways are we different from the AI bots that we create? Is it imagination? Is it free will? Is it the ability to say "no"? Is it emotion?

The biblical narrative highlights the idea that we are "made in the image of God". What does that mean? You could do some research on that phrase, and weave it into your posters—can we create robots in our image, or can we create robots "in the image of God"? (I wonder what they might be able to do/be.) Is being human simply about thinking? Is it to think, therefore to be (a la Descartes?). Is to be human to have not only cognitive ability (thinking), but also physical (a body), emotional and spiritual dimensions? Maybe. (Ava still retains mechanical and electronic parts; and humans can have many parts replaced by mechanical ones. How many artificial parts would a human have to have before we could declare they are not human anymore? Being human is more than just body parts, right? But in what ways?)

By the way, the five questions above were generated by Chat-GPT. Did you guess that? Does that mean ChatGPT can think creatively? Are you less than human if you're responding to a mere computer generated question?

We need to keep chewing on this stuff. I sense there are lots of shades of ethics question in this new frontier of Artificial Intelligence. Hopefully your posters will be a first step in wrestling with it, and also evaluating whether the Turing Test tells us what we really need to know.

Shalom, Mr Kemp.

7

"How would you recognize a Christian?"

Kevin,

The question I'm responding to in this letter is yours: "what the hell are we doing today?" It was a question of surprise as you rumbled into class on Tuesday. I loved your enthusiasm. I hit you with a wall of U2's music. Your incredulity was palpable. A teacher four classrooms down asked me at lunchtime "was that U2 blasting out of your classroom?" "Totally yes" I replied. "Best band ever". Granted, I did have it playing quite loudly over morning interval and hadn't got to the volume button before you started tumbling into class. Everyone else seemed a bit puzzled too when I ignored them and we waited for the song to finish. We weren't exactly rocking it up with *Vertigo*, but hey, how many classes have you had in which you could hear music four rooms away? (U2's genre is mainly post-punk, right?)

    The song was *40*—a melancholic ballad type of song. It's often the song the band now plays at the end of their live shows. But I hope you remember the lesson about Bono. It was kicking off our unit called Cloud of Witnesses, a title taken from the book of Hebrews in the Bible. The idea is that there are a whole bunch of dead (or living) Christians cheering us all on now, particularly in the face of persecution. Probably not quite the unit title in a wealthy private school—who of us has ever experienced persecution for our beliefs? We want to spend some time looking at the question "so what does a Christian actually look like?" How did those who went before us—or older than us—work out their Faith? How would you recognize a Christian? And why would I start with Bono of U2? I listened to U2 solidly over Easter of 2021 because I had five days stuck in my room with Covid 19. I read their *U2 by U2* (2009), and I'm now reading Bono's *Surrender* (2023). Read one of their books and listen to their music at the same time. Awesome.

Anyway: *40* is an interpretation of Psalm 40 in the Bible. We looked at three songs, and unpacked some of the background of Bono and evidence that he is a Christian. We checked out some of his great quotes, and his interview with the Christian theologian Eugene Peterson on YouTube. Here's some of *40*:

> I waited patiently for the Lord
> He inclined and heard my cry
> He lift me up out of the pits
> Out of the miry clay
> I will sing, sing a new song
> How long to sing this song?
> He set my feet upon a rock
> And made my footsteps firm
> Many will see
> Many will see and hear
> I will sing, sing a new song
> How long to sing this song?

Not that singing Psalms from the Bible makes you a Christian. Far from it. Standing in a garage doesn't make you a car. But *Pride (In the Name of Love)*, which we also played and analyzed, picks up on some explicit Jesus imagery: all it takes is one man, even "betrayed with a kiss" (remember Judas?) to effect change, even at great personal risk, like assassination. The song is a tribute to Martin Luther King: "Early morning, April four, Shot rings out in the Memphis sky. Free at last, they took your life." Both Jesus and MLK lived and died for us, "in the name of Love". And then what about *Sunday Bloody Sunday*? Bono and U2 are not afraid to take on the politics of their day, and here, the troubles in Ireland, their home country. That's raw, powerful, confronting hope that justice would break out, peace would be established: there's a long and painful cry—a severe hope—that the horizon will come closer. Again, the Psalms: one third of them are laments, people crying out to God for justice in the face of crippling pain and exploitation.

And if you check out U2's other songs, with Bono in the lead, these themes of hope, peace and justice are sourced from and shaped by Bono's Christian faith, raw and complex as it might be. We saw that in the interview with Eugene Peterson on YouTube I think. He's a bit tired of the church, he does pray to God, values his Christian roots, and then tries to channel this raw passion for Jesus-inspired-justice into the group's songs. Bono doesn't pretend to be nice at all. He's quite open about his own shortcomings in the two books I've read. Like Jesus, I think he would call many of the politicians he's met "vipers" or "white washed tombs"—particularly when he gets worked up about famine in Africa, or the war in Ukraine (which more Christians should get worked up about!).

So I think it's a good way to start our unit on what Christians might look like. We'll land it in a text from Galatians where we are invited to think about "fruit of the Holy Spirit". The proposal is if Christians claim to "have the Holy Spirit", that is, that God's spirit lives in them somehow, then the evidence—the fruit—must be able to be seen. So, love, joy, peace, kindness, goodness, faithfulness, gentleness, self control. Does Bono show these? Do I show these? Will the people, the "cloud of witnesses" we look at in class, show these? That becomes the test I think. If you look at Jesus himself, I think he was pretty unpredictable, brash, a bit rough around the edges. (He took on the priests verbally, hung out with the marginalized and sick and some not-respectables, and upended the money changers' tables in the Temple. Would love to have been there that day!) I reckon he probably looked a bit like Bono—not like the pale white effeminate long haired Renaissance man in the pictures we hang in our churches. I reckon he would have been quite happy to belt out *New Year's Day* with U2 as a resurrection anthem on Easter morning.

Some of the names on the list of people you've chosen to study in your class groups look a bit odd. Some of the very public celebrities who claim to be Christian could do with some close scrutiny of their claims and life style. Look for the "nobodies of this world"—the Kingdom of God is a bit upside-down. The most profound faith is usually found in the most unlikely people (by the standards of society). Use the fruit of the spirit list from Galatians as your benchmark. Bono, I think, has been a good place to start. Unexpected, but good.

> One love. One heart.
> One love, full of mercy.
> Let's join together at the house to pray.
> Let's join together, let's just trust in the Lord.
> One love. Hear my plea.

Shalom, Mr. Kemp.

Claire,

You asked a really tough question in class. Actually I think it wasn't so much a question as a scream of outrage. I agree totally that Christian leaders—Roman Catholic priests, Pentecostal pastors, any in leadership—when they "fall", when they're indicted for abuse or sexual assault, it's just simply wrong. And very wrong. They claim to be Christian, but don't act like one. You should get angry about this! We trust our Christian leaders, and it's with shame I even write about it. These sad cases in the news are simply not what Jesus was about. And the poor kids and women that they've abused. I can sense your outrage. These men do not have the "fruit of the Spirit", which you'd hope would be a moral purity as well. When in leadership, yes, the standards are higher. There is a strong link between inner character and our outer behaviors: we do what we are.

But when I look at the list of the fruit of the Spirit—the evidence of the Holy Spirit in a Christian's life—sometimes I think they are a bit unremarkable. I mean, everyone has some of them, right? Gentleness? Check. Joy? Check. Even love. That sticks them altogether. Maybe God's Spirit is a little bit in each of us already? But perhaps the toughest one is self-control. I think you particularly recognize this as reason for your own outrage: these men have no self-control. So there's some logic here. If someone doesn't have the fruit of the Spirit—the evidence that God's Holy Spirit is in them—then it follows that indeed the Holy Spirit isn't in them, and therefore they probably aren't real Christians. But that is problematic because who are we to judge that? That's probably God's call. Perhaps it's right simply to acknowledge that we are all fallen and ache for redemption. There's a tension in the Kingdom of God where we are both in the image of God but that image is really cracked, like a broken window pane or mirror. We're not as bad as we could be, but we're certainly not as good as we should be.

But it's at this very point of failure and conflict where I think Christians are called to demonstrate peace-making. The ability to make peace is a fruit, I think. Well the list in Galatians has simply "peace" as evidence of the Holy Spirit, like maybe lack of violence, or simply serenity and calmness. Confidence perhaps that God is in control (even when there is immense evil like abuse by those we trust)? But if you flick over to Jesus' own original words in Matthew 5, he has another take on it. He says "blessed are the peace makers . . .". Makers. We in New Zealand have army, navy and air force—we call them the Defence Forces—which we loan to the United Nations as "peace keepers". That's quite different. Our peacekeepers with the UN simply keep two enemy sides apart and stop them scrapping again. Peace, ironically, was gained through guns, and now we keep the two warring factions apart. Sort of like a referee when breaking up a boxing match.

But Jesus calls us Christians not to be peace keepers, but to be peace makers. To actually create, sow, build, and facilitate peace.

To go intentionally into zones of conflict and work to reconcile the two warring factions: to get them to "smoke a pipe" together, to "walk in each other's moccasins", even to "raise each other's children" and serve each other. I think this is where Bono, and Martin Luther King and Jesus himself was at. Jesus washed his disciples' feet. Weird for us, but powerful nonetheless. I once saw this acted out in a very moving way: a Palestinian and a Jew washed each other's feet; a black and a white American washed each other's feet; a man and a woman also. Weighty symbols of Jesus' call to peace-making between individuals representing tribes in conflict. Evidence of a Christian? They intentionally make peace, if we go with Jesus' words, and peace-makers will be called "children of God".

We're going to unpack this more in class. To be a peace-maker, we'll need to do some inner work ourselves on three things. (I got this from my wife who has done a course in international conflict transformation at Eastern Mennonite University in the US.) Firstly we need to "overcome speed"—that is, slow down, take time, be intentional. We need, secondly, to "overcome innocence"—that is, don't be naive, be wise and discerning, look for the deeper nuance in conflict, look to separate symptom from substance. And thirdly, we need to "overcome distance"—we need to actually meet the two warring parties, get them to meet closely, look each authentically in the eye, talk to each other. We'll look at these dynamics in class.

Then we need to also check out three strategies for being peace-makers: being vulnerable, being invitational and being hospitable. If I'm involved in a conflict, then the quickest way to sow peace is to concede my wrong and apologize. (Even if I am right! It's still a good strategy to muster as much humility as possible!) This first step of vulnerability really takes the sting out immediately. Secondly, to be invitational. I mentioned the smoking of a pipe together, the image of men in the Middle East sitting in a circle smoking their shared hookah, the water pipe. And then thirdly hospitable. Make your enemy a meal, invite them around to your place, buy them a beer. This sounds rather simplistic, and we will unpack these more in class. In fact it takes about five periods to really wrestle with hands-on strategies of peace-making. We'll do a case study too, where as a class you will choose a real conflict you regularly experience and work on it to make peace.

So Claire, I'm thinking that if you show even baby steps towards peace-making—how would you do this if you had to sort out the mess of a fallen church pastor and his victims?—then it demonstrates that the Holy Spirit is working in your life. If you check out the other fruit now, they sort of make sense: love, joy, self control, gentleness, they all fold into peace-making too. Vulnerability (humility), invitation and hospitality: do these now when you're in a conflict, or seek to resolve a conflict. And we need peace-makers to step into the breach for these cases of leadership abuse. And if you do, I'd say "the Holy Spirit is working through you". I'm looking forward to these next few weeks reviewing this and exploring how to live fruitfully. First class next week we have a Fruit Auction—how much do you think each fruit of the Spirit is worth and what would you bid? Good fun, but serious stuff follows!

Shalom, Mr Kemp.

Hi again Claire,

I've been sitting here thinking about how disturbed you were—angry!—about those news reports of Christian leaders who had used their position of power to exploit and damage people's lives. Ethics—how we behave and how we make the decisions we do, and how we act out our beliefs, knowing what the right thing to do is—that's so important. And I do think there is a strong connection between who we are and how we behave. What the elephant is standing on will determine whether the friends can reach the fruit, standing on each other's shoulders. Remember that story?

And I've been thinking about that letter I wrote to Kevin, introducing Bono of U2 as a Christian. Many would say he isn't because his beliefs, or at least how he explains (or doesn't explain clearly enough) his beliefs, are different to theirs. Some argue that what you believe doesn't have anything to do with how you behave, citing how they vote at elections: what someone does in private apparently has little to do with how they act in public. I would challenge us, even myself, that what I do in private, when nobody is looking, is the mark of my moral character. There's quite some discussion we could have around that!

So if we're still mulling over what a Christian looks like, or how would I recognize a Christian, as opposed to some other religion or no religion, then checking out the lyrics of the song-writer (Bono, in our example) is probably a good place to start. Songs and poetry reveal the heart. How we act often doesn't align with what we believe because, well, we're all slightly mad, broken, and hopeless individuals, who need help and saving. So I came up with three words (again, I hope you like the alliteration)—belonging, believing and behaving—which might help in identifying who a Christian is, or indeed who anyone is. (Actually they're probably not originally mine. I think I've picked them up somewhere in my reading.)

Belonging: Christians belong in groups. Nothing amazing about that. It's a human need. But this group is called "the Church". The church is, or should be, a place of joy, redemption, healing and destiny. And this belonging-in-the-church is a universal thing (the church universal all over the globe), but also a church, local, here in my neighbourhood. Church keeps you accountable in a community. Churches are communities of "called out ones"—that's what the word actually means. Called out to demonstrate God's love for the world in human relationships, acts of worship and acts of service.

Believing: this is a tricky one. Some people prioritize belief. As long as you believe, then you don't have to worry about how you behave. I don't buy into that. (Believe on Sunday, but do what you like on Monday!) Belief, and good or correct belief, is crucial. The Bible is clear enough what that core of belief is, or should be for a Christian. Keeping the cross and resurrection of Jesus as central in the purposes of God's Kingdom coming. It's captured in ancient creeds—statements generated by the very early church in the face of persecution. Christian belief is Trinitarian (three-in-oneness), Jesus focussed, Bible sourced.

Behaving. Yes, Christian behave in certain ways. They do stuff. If your inner being is changed by the Holy Spirit, then fruit should appear in new actions. Christians aren't just nice, or kind. Some aren't at all! But they experience a new spiritual birth—"born-again"—and then do stuff to enlarge the Kingdom of God, working with the Holy Spirit—continuing Jesus' agenda to offer life in all its fullness to all, but to continue to speak words and do actions that build and interpret each other so that others also can experience this.

I'd argue that all Christians need to be in a church. That's the whole point. A solo Christian is an oxymoron. Behaving, belonging and believing all come together in a place and within a community in which the Holy Spirit inhabits. After the Covid years, when we all got used to doing church on Zoom at home, there was a really slow return to actual in-body church meetings. "Ah, I'll just watch it all on-line at home". But we need to come together. We're compelled to be together. Behaviors are not about following new rules, but following and becoming like Jesus, and gaining new identity by being a follower of Jesus as a member in that community. Notice I haven't put these three "B words" in any order. One doesn't necessarily follow another in any straight sequence. They're all mixed up together. In fact play around with the order. Draw a mind map as to what you think each might look like and how they relate. Quantity and quality of these vary enormously in Christians and in churches. But I'd draw them as three tightly overlapping circles. Recognizing a Christian? All three are happening all the time.

Love to keep this conversation going.

Shalom, Mr Kemp.

8

"Can we really know what (your Christian) God is like?"

Lucy,

How are you going with those short videos on different portrayals of God? You asked how this was all related to Christian Education. You said you hadn't been tuned into movies which implicitly portray God-type characters. Or explicitly. Hollywood offers up so many possibilities. We looked at some in class: Christoph in *The Truman Show* (1998) is a bit of a shocker, I think. Definitely a God-type character, viewing Truman's world and life from above and outside the reality-TV studio set, manipulating Truman and his circumstances for the entertainment of others. A creator, yes, but there is a randomness about Christoph that seems quite unjust. And Morpheus in *The Matrix* (1999)? Morpheus is God-as-a-sparring partner, coach, trainer. I like that. Morpheus is training Neo to become whom Morpheus believes him to be—the ONE (note the anagram!). What about the potential assassin—the voice overlay—in *Phone Booth* (2002)? He seems to be a determinist—he determines the end, depending on what decision Stuart will make. A kind of great cosmic punisher: "do the right thing Stuart and I will reward you. Do bad and you'll get a bullet through your head". It's like the voice demands moral right from Stuart (God is a bully!): "confess your sins, Stuart, and I will spare your life". Ouch.

That survey we did in class about your impressions about God—I'm not surprised at all that many of you (not all!) have this idea that God is a kind of long-bearded white grand-father leaning down over the balcony of heaven. Michelangelo's *Creation of Adam* on the roof of the Sistine Chapel in Rome probably doesn't help. I suspect we've sourced this image from there, and if the critics are right, then that God is stretching out from a place in heaven that looks remarkably like a human brain, perhaps indicating that God is at least the source of mind. But I love that some of you imagine God like Morgan Freeman in *Bruce Almighty* (2003). God is black. Nice. And at least God has a sense of humor, and God is approachable and talking with Bruce. Note Bruce's complaint against God, that God isn't doing his job correctly (theodicy?) and that perhaps Bruce could do it better (Adam and Eve?). And in Year 11 remember when we watched *The Shack*, the Trinity—the three-in-oneness of God (which we'll get onto later) was at least upfront and clear, but the Father was played by a black woman (Octavia Spencer), and then shape shifts into a Native American male healer (Graham Greene), a type of shaman. In the film, Jesus is a Lebanese carpenter and the Holy Spirit (Sarayu) is a female Chinese-Asian. The author/director is playing around with specifically Christian notions of God here.

I don't think in hindsight showing you guys the mojo.com YouTube clip on Hollywood's take on God was actually all that helpful—I might drop it next year. It had God as a deluded and nasty dwarf, a bullying bureaucrat, a 60s hippy, a magician, and so much more across a number of movies. But I was surprised that when I pushed it back to the class for a wider discussion, that you didn't have any more examples. Maybe you're not watching films very critically? I'm thinking The Force in *Star Wars* is a type of god. (I suspect that might be a generation thing: *Star Wars* was a culture shaping phenomenon in my generation, but you guys have moved on!) The Force is monistic and dualistic at the same time: monistic inasmuch as everything is one. Everything in the *Star Wars* universe is infused with The Force, determined by it: not just circumstance, but morality as well. But The Force is also dualistic—it's got a two-ness about it. The Force has a dark side and a light side in equal portions which are opposite to each other. Creator George Lucas is a Buddhist and makes no apology for the Buddhist contours to the films. Perhaps he's made the films' deity deliberately ambiguous?

The other example which comes to mind—and I'm glad Paul named it when I prompted the class—is Eywa in *Avatar* (2009). We watched *Avatar* in Year 9 (and it was a bit tricky extracting key Christian themes out of it, I admit, but it was a fun way to finish the year!). Eywa is the deity, clearly. Being female, she echoes deities from ancient history—many of the ancient gods (think Egypt, Babylon, Assyria, Canaan) were related to fertility, and naturally then, the source of life. And Eywa connects all living things in a vast network through the root system of all the plants on the planet of Pandora, a sort of globally connected consciousness. Animals, and you and I (in avatar form) can bind in with that ponytail-hair connector thing, and listen to the voices of ancestors and the whisperings of the trees. If we wanted a technical name for this type of god, or worldview, it is Animism: Eywa animates—gives life and connects everything. Or is it that all the connections themselves have agency and are called collectively "Eywa"? Either way, I quite like the strong creation and conservation motif here: Eywa is definitely Green! (The whole mining operation on Pandora could then be classified as deicide—the killing of a god.)

But those were just two more examples where I think deity, god, is clear enough in movies. Hollywood continues to create gods for its movies. I'm curious to wonder why. What do you think? (I am also not surprised that some films' heroes are often very close to gods themselves—checkout all those Marvel superheroes! And the Greek, Roman and Scandinavian gods were clearly understood and experienced as deities-as-heroes.) Do you think we're obsessed with finding a god, or needing a god, but not sure what this god might look like, so we keep creating new ones? Or beefing up old ones. Do we need a god to help us make sense of ourselves? To blame when things go wrong? Do we need to be rescued from somewhere higher and more noble than this mundane place? Answers to human dilemmas come from out there, somewhere else, outside this universe: hence our fascination with outer space and alien movies? We want to be rescued; we need an authentic *deus ex machina* salvation.

One last question: if we (or Hollywood) create gods and we give various characteristics to these gods, then these gods are products of our imaginations. That makes them products of our minds. That makes them less than us: our thoughts are products of our minds, and therefore our minds are necessarily bigger than our thoughts. And that means we humans are greater than the gods we create in our minds, which surely makes me, you, us the greater deity right? I am (or you are) God! Did I get that logic right? What do you think? We teased this out in one class—was it yours? I think that if that logic is correct, then the only way to find out about God (which, by definition must be bigger than me, you, us) then that God would have to show us what He/She himself/herself is like, because we are incapable of thinking this God up. God would have to get our attention, have the power and means to communicate with us, and also have the will to. Yes? No?

We finished exploring Hollywood and God by checking out *The Butterfly Circus* (2009). Enough for now. We'll explore that one next letter.

Shalom, Mr Kemp.

Lucy,

"What's an allegory"? We talked about allegories today in class. I'm relieved that the lights went on when it dawned on you that the lion Aslan in *The Lion, the Witch and the Wardrobe* is in fact Jesus. C.S. Lewis makes it plain that his Narnia books are an allegory of the Christian life. Once you can recognize the metaphors in the film, it becomes rather obvious. Or maybe only if you understand Christian faith and theology a bit first? Take the stone table scene:

Aslan has willingly surrendered his life to the witch so that Edmund will go free. (She demanded Edmund's life because Edmund was a traitor.) The witch kills Aslan sacrificially on the stone table in the place of Edmund, and all her demonic hordes celebrate this, thinking they've won! But later, there is a thunderous crack when the stone table breaks and Aslan returns alive, stronger, nobler, renewed to enter into the final battle of Narnia, having bet on a deeper magic in Narnia that death does not hold a willing and innocent victim who has died on behalf of another person (that is, Aslan for Edmund). This is allegory: a story told using different characters in a different universe to reveal some hidden meaning. If you unpick the story, it is definitely the Jesus event and particularly the cross and resurrection that mirrors the Christian story. (As an aside, I love Lucy's assessment of Aslan—Jesus by implication—when she says to Tumnus: "He's not a tame lion, but he is good".)

Similarly, C.S. Lewis' friend J.R.R. Tolkien works Christian themes into his trilogy of *Lord of the Rings*, but more subtly, and you can't really tease out any one event or character that is God or Jesus or the devil like Lewis did. Evil is real enough in *LOTR* (seeking to be embodied in Sauron), but the power for good—all things pertaining to God—is spread across Frodo, Gandalf and Aragorn (servant, priest and king?). We'd have to devote the whole year to exploring these. Maybe we should!

But for lack of time, and also because it's a great short film, we watched *The Butterfly Circus*. We finished our unit on "God at the movies" with this film because again, it's a great allegory. You guys didn't pick this up immediately in class, but that's OK, because that is what class is for—to explore the possibilities, to look critically at the culture and the claims that are put to us.

Once you get over the shock of realising that Will in *The Butterfly Circus,* played by Nick Vujicic, actually has no arms or legs in real life (it's not CGI'd), then I think the allegorical themes come through powerfully. I like the activity we did where you all had to choose to identify with one of the main characters, and explain why: Anna (the ex-prostitute); Poppy (the old guy begging); George (the violent ex-pub brawler), Mendez, the circus master, and of course, Will. Great discussion. And particularly when you recognized that the film is deliberately naming four stereotypical groups of people on the margins: Anna (sex worker), Poppy (elderly), George (violent man), and Will (disabled). But it is Mendez who is the god-figure—or probably more the Jesus of the film. And three of you wanted to be Mendez. Once I'd suggested that Mendez might be a Jesus-like figure, you came up with a list of his characteristics that justified this suggestion: prioritizes the individual, sees the best in people, gathers in the people on the margins, brings joy to everyone, is generous, respects people's choices, gives meaning, invitational, leads, heals, uses the power of words for positive results, builds community, invests himself with odd people, accepts people first just as they are, is non-judgemental. You could probably pick out a few more Jesus-like qualities. Thanks to the class for all those contributions! If you took your list of qualities and compared it to one of the gospels, I think you'd be quite justified. (What's missing, that would conclusively persuade us that Mendez is Jesus, would be if Mendez was executed—willingly laid his life down—on behalf of this band of misfits, so that they then find meaning and success, and their salvation was due to this willful self-offering of Mendez—like Aslan and Jesus. But you can push an allegory only so far for the plot to still work!)

If Mendez is all of these things, then this rag-tag bunch whom he is shaping into a meaningful community (a Butterfly Circus) is a picture of the church. Yes, you read that right. The circus is like the church. They follow Mendez. Christians in their strange communities (churches) follow Jesus. And the church should be a community of rescued people (isn't that what Mendez is doing?) which is healed, forgiven, renewed, and following its leader (Jesus). The butterfly image is a common one in Hollywood—indeed throughout our culture generally—to signify new birth, changes for the good, renewal, new life, potential, hope. Remember it appears in *Patch Adams* (1998) which we watched in Year 12 when Patch decides not to take his own life, but to turn from throwing himself off the cliff and start afresh. God answers Patch's prayer through the appearance of a butterfly.

How Far Down Does the Elephant Go?

This is one clear theme in *The Butterfly Circus*—that Mendez rescues people on the margins—they don't go looking for him. He finds them. Then he shows them who he is by inviting them into this new community and gives them meaning there by recognizing, affirming and training them in what they're good at, in skills that they never knew they had. I think this is a pretty good picture of who God might be: God reveals (that's a Christian word now)—shows himself to us, and invites us to follow, through the life of Jesus. *The Butterfly Circus* imagines us into what the Kingdom of God might look like. I think we're on more stable ground there than the speculations around Hollywood's other gods. God is able and willing to show himself to us, through Jesus. Thoughts?

Shalom, Mr Kemp.

Anita,

This three-in-oneness idea that us Christians claim is the Christian God of the Bible I concede can be a bit of a head spinner. "How can God be one and three at the same time?" Fair question. From your own Hindu background in India, I know you have the idea that deity can appear in different forms: Vishnu appears in ten different avatars. But the biblical God is really different. The Trinity is always the Trinity: Father, Son and Holy Spirit. I know in *The Shack*, when we watched it last year the author has these three as quite distinct, and implies (actually shows us at one point) that at least God the Father seemed to have some sort of dominance in the trio. God the Father is initially a woman (for that is how Mac needed to experience Him), then morphs into a man. (Again, "I think you'll need a father for what we need to do today", He—Elousia/Papa—says, appearing as a Native American shaman/healer). But you need to remember that *The Shack* is a novel, and the author is quite clear on that, and so we shouldn't get our definitive beliefs and theology from it.

But throughout the Bible this trinity is never explained. It's not even really mentioned. It's assumed. Different parts of the Bible talk of the Father; also the son—Jesus—is clearly a male in time and place and history; and also the Holy Spirit is like a wind (spirit and wind are the same word in the original languages) and some claim that the Holy Spirit can be thought of as female (because *ruach* is a feminine word in Hebrew). But at no point do any of the Bible writers say "now I'm going to explain this God to you". The Bible, you'll remember, is written mainly as story, more in sunrise-sunset language. Much of it is from our viewpoint, from our experience of this God and how this God reveals Himself to us over time. (Ah, the male pronoun! English language doesn't serve us well when speaking about God.) The Bible is like us watching what this God is doing, and then trying to write down our understanding of the outcomes of God's involvement in history, culture and our lives, a long and twisting story over 66 books.

Plot spoiler: no one through all the 2,000 odd years of Christianity has really got their heads around this Trinity thing. Again, like the Hollywood gods, if we could, then Trinity might be reduced to something less than us, making me greater (that is, God). I think it's good we don't really understand God—God is a mystery. You know this well from your own Hindu background. But to really anchor God down—maybe God knows that we need to have something concrete—Christians claim we know God in the person of Jesus, a real man walking and breathing amongst us in real time and place for 33 odd years in the area which is now Israel, Lebanon and Palestine. At Jesus' baptism all three members of the Trinity come together—a voice from the Father from above, Jesus the man in the river Jordan, and the Holy Spirit appearing as a dove: three, but one. In effect Jesus says this: if you want to know the Father, know me. I and the Father are one. And when I leave, the Holy Spirit will continue what I've been doing: the Holy Spirit is me in spirit form. No wonder the locals of the day killed him—you can't go around claiming you are God. Unless of course you are, and there's a resurrection to endorse it. Like C.S. Lewis suggests, Jesus is a liar, a lunatic, or who he claims to be, Lord.

I was talking to Ishmael the other day, and he said that in Islam, they think our Christian God is three distinct gods. Like we worship three gods. (I conceded here that *The Shack* doesn't particularly help us with this question—at least at first viewing). I know that Muslims accuse Christians of losing our right to claim Monotheism (God is one), because of this notion of Trinity. But this three-ness—I pointed this out to him—is firmly embedded in early Jewish proclamations that God is one: "Hear, oh Israel. The Lord, the Lord, He is One. Worship only him". We hold strongly to the one-ness of God and the three-ness of God at the same time. It's not roles (like I'm a dad, father and uncle at the same time), nor are they distinct (three different gods), nor do they have three functions (creator, redeemer, and life giver): it's like three persons held tightly together by the bond of love. We might see or experience only one at work at some time, but all three are there together when one is. Water in three states (ice, liquid, steam)? A three leaf clover? I know, I know. It's all a bit of a mystery. But that may well be the point. Start with Jesus. That's the door in.

Shalom, Mr Kemp.

9

"Why are there so many different religions in the world?"

Anita,

Picking up this conversation with Ishmael again this week and he continued wanting to talk about the world religions. We have a good number of Hindus at school, some Muslim families, about six Jewish students, quite a few Buddhists, plus some Baha'i, and the number of Sikhs is increasing too. You can tell the Sikh boys because they tie their hair up in a man-bun with a *rumal*, the head cloth. (They take a vow not to cut their hair.) So we actually moved on from the nature of God—Ishmael had quite a bit to say about Allah and whether Allah in Islam is the same as the God of Christianity (YHWH by name). But he did ask the simple question of why are there so many religions in the world. And I've got that question up on the wall in our classroom. Did you notice I change the question every week?

It's a great question. And an important one. Why are there so many different religions in the world? Or, why are there so many, and why are they different? And what is religion anyway? So there's quite a bit "just under the surface" with this question. Thanks for keeping the question alive.

So let's start with this last question: what is religion anyway? It's perhaps an unsettling question here in New Zealand because we like to think of ourselves as non-religious. There's no official state religion, and census figures every five years show more and more people who are "not-religious" or something similar. Even here at this school, a church school no less, I find many students for whom religion *per se* is not on their radar, nor see any reason why it should be. At least, that's what they say. And alarmingly nor do they realize that all these new immigrants here in New Zealand do actually value their own religions, and that there are a whole bunch of religions growing in New Zealand that are not part of the old mainstream Christianity (Anglican, Catholic, Presbyterian, Methodist, Baptist) that came with the original colonizing immigrants. We seem to pride ourselves in being secular non-religious, although I suspect we really have little idea what that actually means, nor how adherence to a religion might benefit us in some way.

So religion. At no point in our Christian Education syllabus do we actually define what a religion is. Actually we have a nod towards a definition in about lesson 4 of Year 9, I think. But that's all. I think we just assume that Christianity—or how the school's denomination of Presbyterianism sees the world—is self evident, or even that it isn't a religion but something else. (It's tempting to say Christianity is rather a "relationship with Jesus". I'd agree, but it seems a bit simplistic at this point, so we'll put that definition aside for now.) I have to give you some input here: we haven't looked at any of this in class. We can start with thinking about religions as having "family resemblances". The philosopher Ludwig Wittgenstein came up with this phrase. There are some things in common across the whole spectrum of religions. So for example, in both your Hinduism and my Christianity we recognize acts of worship to a god or gods. There are initiation and washing rituals. There are heroes and heroines whom we praise who embody our religion to a high quality. Stuff like that. Family resemblances: they're

Why are there so many different religions

different, but they are recognisably similar, like how you and your brother or sister look similar.

Actually, full confession. I've written a book about all this, and it's on the bookshelf down the back of the classroom. *The One-Stop Guide to World Religions* (Oxford: Lion, 2013). If you check out pages 8 and 9, you'll see I reference a list of core characteristics of religion by a professor called Ninian Smart who wrote a book about it all in 1989. He reckons that if we try and define a religion, then we should recognize seven contours, or "dimensions". These are descriptions. You can go and read them if you like. However, I've got my own definition (and I'm quoting from page 8 of my book) which will help us better, I think, in trying to answer Ishmael's question of why there are different religions (and so many):

> Religion is a quest for an ideal existence, a seeking beyond oneself for meaning in life. Some say that the quest itself defines what religion is: others that the quest has both an end and an answer. Most (but not all) religion claims some knowledge of and relationship with the divine, or the spiritual, or gods, or an ultimate God. Religion takes shape in rituals, beliefs and institutions: worship, community, the writing and compiling of scriptures—these give order and shape to identity, communities, and experiences of the divine. Religion regulates ethics: it answers the question 'How should I live?' Some religions are shaped by circumstances and their moment in history. Others claim to be revelations—the god reveals characteristics, codes for living, even personality to humans.

International research, like by the Pew foundation, consistently reminds us that around 84% of the world is religious, or is part of a formal religion. (Check out their webpage for details: pewresearch.org.) Obviously it's difficult to measure (what are we measuring?), but in short, it's a myth that religion per se is dying or God is dead or that science has got rid of religion or some such. Humans, I think, are incorrigibly religious. We can't help ourselves. We want something, someone, to fill a spiritual void we often perceive in our lives. Blaise Pascal called this a "God-shaped vacuum" inside us. In year 13 we look at worldviews and at the beginning of the unit I take a survey as to which one of ten questions each of the students think is the most important. For 2022 and 2023, 96 students did this survey (over six classes). The two highest tallies were: "what is my purpose in life?" (31) and "what happens when we die?" (23).

In other words, over half my year 13 students (54 of them) thought that either of these two questions is the most important for them. The other eight questions received no more than 9 responses each. Combining these numbers with other literature on worldview, we came to the conclusion that humanity has two basic questions we need answering: who am I (identity—what is my purpose, what am I doing here, now, alive?), and where am I going (destiny—where am I going in life, but also after I die, if anywhere. What happens next)? In essence this affirms the two questions my year 13s prioritized. Religion—any religion, answers questions we have, and fills gaps we perceive. And it could be spiritual gaps, psychological gaps, identity gaps, relational gaps, intellectual gaps. Well all of this, but more.

Apart from our own quest to fill gaps, there are other reasons there are religions. Someone claims to have a vision or extraordinary insight, and tells and persuades people who believe him/her, and a following emerges (Islam, Mormonism). Some religions claim to be fulfilments of what came before (Christianity, Buddhism). Some are protests and renewal movements: some religions form for political reasons. (Henry VIII's establishment of Anglicanism; Presbyterianism in Scotland didn't want bishops, because bishops were English and Anglican, simply put.) This means that some religions are tied to a polity (a country) and culture and therefore located in certain places: Lutheranism in Germany and Scandinavia, Hinduism in India, Confucianism in China, Yoruba in Africa, Mormonism in Utah. Often religion isn't too organised at all, like it's a response to how a tribe's unique location plays out: their religion explains things like storms, rain, fertility of the plants, movements of animals they hunt and the likes. We don't need to doubt people's sincerity in all these religions: people really do see the world differently, write about it, bring order to their writings and behaviors. For your own Hinduism, I have no doubt at all that people have good reason to commit to a religion undergirded by karma. If you accept certain assumptions, then karma makes a lot of sense. It offers a way for understanding the two key needs we have of identity and destiny.

But what about belief? The guts of the core philosophy or theology of a religion? Are we all simply worshipping the same God? Are all these religions just different paths up the same mountain? The Dalai Lama (head of Tibetan Buddhism) talks about religions as the five fingers on the hand, connected to the palm. I've heard him say it. I'd want to know what he thinks the palm is—some sort of commonality? Are religions connected just because of "family resemblances" or do they, according to the Dalai Lama, fundamentally have the same substrate (the palm)?

Another book on my bookshelf at the back of our classroom is one by Stephen Prothero, called *God is Not One: The Eight Rival Religions that Run the World—and why their Differences Matter* (New York: HarperOne, 2010). Prothero was a prof at Boston University. I think this book is brilliant because it gives licence to us all to have a conversation where we actually admit what we've thought all along. Maybe this was behind Ishmael's question, that no, it is not the same deity sitting on top of the mountain, and no, the finger/palm model of the Dalai Lama doesn't work, because each of the religions is actually competing. Their beliefs are different, and they all think they are the correct one. Prothero names them on the cover as "rivals"!

OK. This letter's getting a bit long. More next time.

Shalom, Mr Kemp.

Ishmael,

You'll see I picked up your question with Anita, the question about why there might be so many religions in the world. I hope you're able to read that. I'm loving the conversation because firstly, you're asking the question (which not too many students actually care about, realistically), and secondly it represents your genuine engagement with big horizon stuff, which students (especially teenagers) could be doing earlier!

I want to continue on that other question we started talking about—whether Allah of Islam and the God of Christianity are the same. Or step back for a bigger view—whether all paths lead up the same mountain from different sides to find the same God sitting on the top, that is, are all the religions just the same, and we all worship the same God? It certainly is trendy these days to be tolerant—like if we even talk about some things that might be controversial, well that's totally un-cool, because it implies someone might be wrong and we all take offence too easily these days. I think also we avoid the conversation because if we come to the conclusion that any one of the claimants to being the right (or true) religion wins, then people will be confronted by this, they may have to change! In other words, there are implications for the discussion, particularly if we hold to religion chiefly being about identity and destiny. What if I've betted on the wrong horse? Allah and the Christian God YHWH (remember, I said this is pronounced something like "Yahweh". No one quite knows how to say God's name as it appears in the Bible simply as four letters. But it morphed into "Jehovah". In most Bibles YHWH transliterated into LORD)—they are prime candidates for being the same because they both belong to monotheistic religions. One God. Are they the same God?

I pointed Anita in the direction of Prothero's book *God is not One*. (It's on my bookshelf at the back of the classroom). Well no guessing what Prothero thinks. No, they're not the same. And they can't be. Before you read Prothero's book though, just stop to think about some potential differences between Allah and YHWH (and similarities?). Both Islam and Christianity are mono-theistic (they believe there is only one God—but is it the same God?). Both have a prophet who is key: Muhammed in Islam, and Jesus in Christianity. Actually, both honor a line of prophets, and in some cases, the same prophets. Both acknowledge holy scriptures (the Qur'an for Islam and the Bible for Christianity). And we could do these elementary lay-man's comparisons with any religion. Buddhism, for example, doesn't technically have a god it acknowledges (although once you check out Buddhism's spread, lots of local deities make it into Buddhism in different forms!). So just stopping, pausing and looking at what's going on is a good start.

But Prothero here is now really helpful. I like the way he's offered to us a clear argument declaring that no, the religions are seriously different and that these differences matter. I actually wrote a review of the book some years ago, in a journal called *Encounters* (Issue 46. September, 2013). Much of what follows comes out of that review.

Prothero's genius in his book is the very simple notion that not all religions claim to be dealing with the same problem, and therefore they offer different solutions. The book is divided into eight chapters—one religion for each—with an end section on Atheism in a ninth chapter. (Is Atheism a religion? It certainly has some "family resemblances" with religion.) So, for Islam, the problem is pride; the solution is submission. (Would that be right, from your experience?) For Confucianism, the problem is chaos; the solution is social order. (A side note here: I understand that Confucius' teaching was chiefly civic, that is, how to order society. It's where we get the strong Chinese notions of filial piety, honoring your parents.) For Buddhism, the problem is suffering; the solution is awakening. For Judaism, the problem is exile; the solution is return to God. For Hinduism, the problem is bondage to *samsara* (a cyclical time-space regulated by *karma*); the solution is *moksha* (release). We could bring Anita in to check if that resonates with her. For Christianity, the problem is sin; the solution is salvation. (This is certainly true, but I'd say it's possibly more nuanced than that.) In West African Yoruba the problem is that we have forgotten our destiny; the solution is to remember our destiny.

So I think this is helpful to explain why there are different religions: they are the product of us trying to name what's wrong with the world, and then offering a solution to that very problem. If religions offer answers to our questions about identity and destiny, I think possibly they go beyond Prothero's categories, and each is ultimately trying to answer one question: what about death? That's perhaps why I defended my question posted on the wall the other day when Tracey told me she thought it was a bit gloomy to have a question about death on the side wall of the classroom. But it's the ultimate question. Prothero thinks religions are trying to "ward off the chill of death". Monique in your class had a similar insight: "I think religion's purpose is to lessen the fear of the unknown: like there were too many questions and people who wanted answers, so religion was created as a way to ebb the fear".

But I think there's another question that comes before Prothero's or Monique's insights: how well can I live now, before death? How can I flourish now, here, today, in this place, before I die? Identity before destiny. Or rather, destiny is determined by my identity. My answer will be determined by my question. If I'm persuaded that a god or God is part of the solution—if I'm a theist—then who I am becoming (identity) is shaped by the God in whom I believe (who gives me identity), which will determine my destiny.

Ultimately which religion we each choose should adequately answer those tough questions we have, and do so consistently and convincingly. You need to be satisfied that the answers your religion offers deal to identity and destiny in meaningful, helpful, realistic, and empowering ways. I'm a Christian and will remain so because I've come to experience that when Jesus said "I have come to give you life, and life in all its fullness", I've started to experience this on this side of death, and because of Jesus' resurrection, I'm confident I'll experience it even more so on the other side of death.

Catch-up with Monique and have a read of Prothero. Actually, I think Peter borrowed it. I'll let you know when it's back so you can have a read. Somewhere tucked in amongst this letter is implicit answers to whether Allah and YHWH are the same. Explicitly: no. I don't think so. Because Islam and Christianity pose different root causes of the problem with humanity, then the personality of their Gods are different. In my experience, Muslims want to talk about Allah, but Christians want to talk about Jesus (at that level alone there seems to be quite a difference). Ultimately, from these conversations I've had with other Muslims, it seems there is an issue with Christian claims over who Jesus is. But I do think it would serve us all well to read each other's holy books, and keep talking!

Shalom, Mr Kemp.

Richard,

That discussion we had in class was really important. The class was testing out which churches were appropriate to visit for your church visit assignment. We accepted all the mainline ones: Anglican, Presbyterian, Methodist, Baptist, Catholic, Salvation Army, Brethren and the Pentecostal ones (Elim, Assembly of God, Apostolic) and the newer ones like Vineyard. And each of these denominations—remember that word from Year 9?—has its own smaller groupings for a variety of reasons. The value of your visit to different churches is we can then compare them all, seeing what they have in common and in what ways they are different and does that matter.

Then you tossed in your question—and it's a timely one!—"what's the difference between a religion and a cult?" Each year this always provokes an awkward conversation because we drop the Jehovah's Witnesses and the Latter Day Saints—the Mormons—from the list of possible church visits. At face value they look Christian-ish, but are they? And what would be the criteria for judging? And inevitably someone says "what about Gloriavale—that community on the West Coast of the South Island?", because that's been in the news on and off for years, and people call it a cult. Or is Gloriavale a mainline Christian denomination that simply chooses to explore how to do Christianity differently? And how would you know? And we allow Seventh Day Adventists, but nobody visits their churches because they meet on Saturdays.

So where do we go with this question? What's the bigger picture? Is it even important? I think the best place to start is to take some heat out of the question, and acknowledge that when we're talking about "cults", we're usually thinking of "Christian cults", that is, smaller religious movements that come out of, or have reacted against Christianity. Would Hindus use the word "cult" to describe any of their internal "denominations"; would Muslims?

Perhaps. But even then—take the Hare Krishnas, for example—they definitely look Hindu, but I remember talking with Hindu friends in Connaught Circus in New Delhi (the heart of the city) who were standing around watching the Hare Krishnas dancing and singing, who volunteered that they were "weird, not Hindu, and a Western invention".

So maybe that could be our first two big ideas: "cults" are often new expressions of old religions (we usually see them as influenced somehow by Christianity, but there are others), and more often than not, explicitly Western expressions. Vast numbers of books have been written about "cults", and the term is really pejorative now. It has been nuanced—particularly through the 1960s and 1970s—as mind-bending, manipulative, coercive, deceptive, delusionary. Anti-cult movements have sprung up to "rescue" people from them, and "deprogram" people. And there was some urgency to these rescues because some of the cults ended up in mass suicides. And some of the people rescued were really messed up. Sociologists love studying these cults because, well, they're fairly self contained (a distinct place, a definite number, clear ideological edges, orderly beliefs, a charismatic leader, specific named and sometimes shocking or tragic events in their history) and because some of them are just weird and so, so different.

Having said that, there is a move today away from the pejorative term "cult". We now talk of New Religious Movements (NRMs) or Alternative Religious Movements. This takes the sting out of the brain-washing accusation, and granted, there are stories now of people who choose to leave, don't return, and with assistance, manage to integrate back into mainstream society. These NRMS tend to draw on a wider spectrum of beliefs—maybe this is our third big idea—in fact many are a potpourri of beliefs and practices, even a DIY type of religion: and they often now are classified back into mainstream religion according to standard definitions. Would "Flat-Earthers" be considered a cult, or just a quirky pseudo-Science? Any weekend New Age fair is a great walk through of these NRMs and you can see what they now look like. And they tend to be commercialized. They sell stuff: sell experiences, sell books, sell instruction manuals, sell biographies and memoirs, sell ideas. Alas, the commodification of religion!

But there is still some of the "cult" category around. Maybe big idea number four might be around the solo charismatic leader, accountable to no-one but himself (and yes, usually it's a male). Look for that. Mainstream churches will always have some sort of institutional accountability—a bishop or superintendent, a committee, a board, an annual or quarterly congregational meeting, a legal status accountable to the government. (Like a "state" religion, some have Acts of Parliament that partially govern them.) Cults usually have solo charismatic dictatorial, often manipulative, leaders. In fact when a religious group's leadership starts going this way—usually justifying some sexual or power grab—then it's time to get out!

And then there's the stuff a cult believes—what it holds to be true, and how it sees the world. This is their "doctrine"—the fifth idea (if we're counting still). This is why the Jehovah's Witnesses and the Mormons (the Church of Jesus Christ of the Latter Day Saints) are sometimes classified as "cults". Their doctrines simply do not line up with the rest of the Christian denominations; the heart core of the Faith is just different. These unique beliefs are often offered as "updates" or "new revelation" given by some divine messenger or some insight or intuition of the founder, or new texts that are put up as authoritative, that supersede the Bible. Like we talked about in class a little—I'd classify the Mormons and JWs as "on the edges of Christianity". The rest of the Christian denominations can't embrace their core beliefs, chiefly around their view of the Bible, and in particular who Jesus is and what Jesus taught and his significance. This I think is different to say the Seventh Day Adventists: some have historically classified them as a cult, but not these days. The SDAs have some unique understandings about Sabbath (the 7th day of rest) and the second coming of Jesus (the Advent), but these are more idiosyncrasies, like the Pentecostals could be accused of overemphasising the Holy Spirit or the Anglicans could be accused of prioritizing the Prayer Book rather than the Bible.

How Far Down Does the Elephant Go?

I think in the end the big test of difference between religion and cult might be the answer to the question: "how free are you to leave"? Cults will often demand a total embrace—money, house, family, commitment to all that the group is offering. A member's identity is subsumed totally into the bigger group's. Often a cult is really aggressive in its recruiting. A religion should grow you into a better person, but a cult will shrink you into conformity. It is so hard then to actually leave, as the community becomes all you've ever known: you may even have changed your name! A religion may put this pressure on you too—there is much discussion (and new laws in some countries too!) around conversion between religions—but I'd argue that the individual is still free to keep their autonomy and self determination, even if they have to undergo some suffering or trauma when they convert. That pressure is most often seen when the religion and the culture are tightly woven together, like Islam or Hinduism or Tibetan Buddhism or Judaism. Leaving the religion is often perceived as "leaving your culture" or "leaving your family" or "denying your identity/country", and some converts pay a huge price for this.

Anyway. There is a truckload of material written about cults and religions and their relationship. Not all of it is helpful, and much of it is simplistic and reduces definitions to sound bites. We all believe something—our elephants are standing on something—and we all need to be in some sort of human community. We all have some autonomy and should be free to embrace the worldview and religion that we think makes the best sense of everything. So when you do your church visit keep these big ideas in mind. The whole assignment ends up with a really interesting full-on class discussion about what exactly do the churches have in common, and where are they different and why.

Shalom, Mr Kemp.

Paige and Morgan,

Wow. That was quite the conversation. I hope you explained to your next class teacher why you were so late. I had a free period and could keep chatting, but maybe I should have given you a late pass for your next class. Hope you politely explained why we took a good thirty minutes of extra Christian Ed time!

I think you were trying to shock me. It's not every day I have two students stand in front of me and declare themselves to be Satanists. I loved the conversation that followed though—maybe you were simply pushing the boundaries? And you should, because what is school for if you can't put those big identity forming questions out there and explore them? So I hope you found our conversation as stimulating as I did. And no I didn't freak out. I've met and talked with Satanists before. What I found curious was that I ended up telling you more about what Satanism is about than you yourselves had understood!

Declaring this at the end of a Christian Ed class was perfect timing. I heard you say or imply something like "this Christian stuff is all very well, and Jesus is awesome, but we find Satanism more meaningful". Like many of these conversations, I detect you were asking a question, rather than making a statement, more like: "Sir, we're exploring other worldviews and Satanism contrasts so obviously with Christianity, so what do you think?"—even a bit of rebel in you?

So can we keep this conversation going? I wouldn't be surprized if I'm the first Christian who's given you this invitation. Satan doesn't get a good rap in Christianity, obviously. So there are two things we need to unpack—and I guess I'm going over here what we talked about after class.

With Satanists I've talked to and books I've read, I understand that Satanists accuse Christians of creating Satan, that Satan is in fact a Christian invention, and this image—the guy in the red tights with horns, hairy legs, cloven hooves and a pitchfork—is what the Bible offers. However, this image is more an amalgam of different images through Christian and pre-Christian history, embedded in our culture perhaps by images from Dante's *Inferno*, the first part of his *Divine Comedy* (~1321). The word Satan is indeed in the Bible: it has roots back into ancient Hebrew, and then translated into the Greek of the New Testament. Essentially it has the idea of "accuser", and usually put up as a spiritual being who has agency in opposition to Jesus specifically or God more generally. (Etymologically, the word "satan", while generally meaning "accuser", also contains the idea of the "prosecutor", like in a court of law: the D.A. in America, or the Crown prosecutor in the British legal system.)

So yes Satan is associated with evil, death, destruction, opposition, temptation, and embodied in the snake of the Garden of Eden and various shadowy figures (often Emperors and their empires) throughout the Bible and then the serpent in the last book, Revelation. It's a word often paralleled with *demon* or *diabolic* or "the demonic" drawing on the Greek translation of the Hebrew. In the Bible, Satan is regarded as a fallen angel, nothing more. So Satan is not in dualistic opposition to Jesus. While only a "fallen angel", the Bible nevertheless does concede quite some power to Satan ("prowling around like a roaring lion" for example), but he is a being whose days are numbered, Jesus having stripped him of power at the resurrection. So, yes, Satan/the devil is totally a Christian thing, but the horned hairy-leg goat-like guy in red tights is more the result today of the over-active imaginations of European authors and Hollywood directors.

But your Satanism is *not* into this Satan. The Satanism that you are exploring is quite different. It's generally grouped into a New Age type of classification, a New Religious Movement that is shaped by similar motivations: the search for meaningful personal identity, personal freedoms (you highlighted this when you said it's about the notion of "do what thou wilt"), and a revolt against organized religion (and hence offers a radical framework for a different morality and ethical decision making). If you research back say 500 years, you'll find its roots in the idea of inversion: turning Christian Faith (Catholic, back then) upside down, and in doing this mocking it through parody. But modern Satanism dates from the founding of the Church of Satan in 1966 by Anton La Vey (1930–1997)—and it does not believe in or promote a literal, existing, volitional, spiritual being. LaVey went on to publish *The Satanic Bible* in 1969 and founded various rituals that are now practiced. It's a sort of secular metaphorical idea of the alleged qualities of Satan. So therefore there is no being that Satanists actually worship. They are not "devil worshippers". Christians "read" Satanism wrongly at this point—they assume the Satan of Satanism is the same Satan of the Bible, and hence a being that demands allegiance and worship. But even this short history—their use of "church" and "Bible" gives you an idea of inversion—you can see the tipping of Christianity particularly on its head and mocking it. Your Satanism is really into archetypes (check out the philosopher Carl Jung on this)—choosing the more generic qualities of our human ideals and personifying them, giving them agency, like individualism (or "antinomianism"—being against rules), a certain anti-herd mentality, rationality, and self indulgence. There are some really tough "inverted" notions in your Satanism that you need to name: LaVey's nine core principles are certainly antithetical to Christianity. You'd have to do some research to make sure you understood these.

Ironically, it's in the very nature of what LaVeyan Satanism promotes that has some real discussion points with Christianity. And I'd encourage you to think through these carefully. Both Satanism and Christianity explore what it means to be free. Satanism promotes personal indulgence, life without rules, prioritising the pleasures of self. Jesus' notions of freedom are the opposite: denying oneself to the point of self-sacrifice for others—"laying your life down". Both Satanism and Christianity ask the question "what does the ideal human look like?" Particularly the ideal man. Christianity has much to say about us being made "in the image of God", broken as it is, but the ideal "image of God" is in fact Jesus. No surprises there with that claim.

I'd advise you to tread carefully. You will find lots of overlap with other New Agey types of beliefs and communities. Witchcraft and Wicca hold hands with Satanism. But I think, like any mainstream religion, or New Religious Movement, or any more generic worldview, you need to keep your eyes wide open, engage critically, and have the courage to accept what you can and reject what you must. Last week I was supervising a Year 13 exam study session, and we all started chatting about these big issues (which was much more interesting than Physics and French verbs), and one student announced: "I'm a Pagan". I reckon she was doing what you two did: trying to shock me, which I wasn't, but hey, again, what are we talking about, let's clear the lens a bit and see what we're actually saying and where it might go.

If we went back to Prothero's framework (remember that book on my bookshelf at the back of the classroom)—as humans we're just wrestling with how to make sense of this crazy life we live. We know there's a lot of good around, but we experience the world as seriously screwed up, and death particularly is a puzzle. How we "live fully" will be a question we hold all our lives. How we wrestle with these questions—well, you did a wise thing: keep talking, keep thinking, keep seeking what's true and noble. And my counsel to you on your Satanism is what I'd also counsel to others who are looking at any one of the New Religious Movements that are out there that shout for our attention: stay alert, stay critical, keep talking openly about how your beliefs are shaping up, keep yourself accountable in your own network of people you know and respect.

Shalom, Mr Kemp.

10

"Isn't it all just 'meant to be'?"

Kieren,

Nice wandering around during lunchtime duty chatting the other day. Our conversation certainly made duty a bit more interesting than normal. I sensed though that you really didn't have much idea about the conversation that happened in class last week when Kylie, Will and Hamish got going about *karma*. No doubt it sounded quite strange, particularly when they got so animated! I saw you listening intently before you threw in your own question.

We hear the word "karma" a lot these days. It's sneaked into English (and is mainstreamed now in the language, I think), but it definitely has Asian roots, from Hinduism and the traditions of India. When I lived in India, karma and related concepts were in the air we breathed. In Hinduism it is a well developed idea with lots of scriptural context. For example, the *Gita*, probably Hinduism's most popular poem, explores karma as "action", a principle where every event is both cause and effect, coupled with moral responsibility and culpability, or duty. But it's used in a bit of an undisciplined way in Western and English speaking contexts I think, which regrettably is not uncommon for a number of appropriated words that have sprouted in English. I remember Boy George's song with the repeating lyrics "karma karma karma chameleon, you come and go, you come and go". That dates me I guess—1983? 1984? If you look around in our cultural motifs, you'll find it soon enough: karma is a catch all word that connotes inevitability. The result is inevitable: cause and effect. It's inescapable that the consequences of my choice were such and such. Or luck came to me because of my karma. Or somehow some law of the universe is acting favourably on my behalf. In short (although a bit simplistically) karma is something like "do good and you'll get good; do bad and you'll get bad". The "come and go" bit in Boy George's song implies a circularity: "what goes round comes round", or "what will be will be". You may have heard these phrases? (Boy George's song—Culture Club's actually—is possibly more about alienation, but even so, woven through the song is a sense of action and consequences). Anand asked me recently: "Why are people judged [by God]? What if someone has done equal amounts of good and bad?" It's quite common I think for people to think that if they've done enough good stuff—the income on that side of the ledger—then it's an automatic ticket into heaven (or the reward for whatever happens next, after death). People's understanding of karma usually defaults to believing they have lots of "good karma".

Will, Hamish and Kate had folded into their argument some other things too. Hamish got defending the Greek gods! And he wasn't too fazed when Kate reminded him how fickle and random they were. (I think Kate's studying Classics.) Will was seriously into fate: everything is pre-determined. We have no choices. No free will. Life is all mapped out for us, and we have no real influence on the path destined for us by fate. Will appealed mainly to genetics: you can't choose your parents, and everything is in your genes, and we are the products of material evolution that is driven by genetic fitness, time, and a certain randomness. Kate reminded the boys that so much of their own privilege was determined by the wealth of their parents, and that we were still living off the benefits of inherited wealth from British colonial exploitation of New

Zealand which we had no control over as we are four or so generations removed from then. Fate dictates so much, they concluded.

So listening in, I was left really with the one big question: who or what is actually running this universe? Is it karma, fate, God, luck? Why are we who we are? Are we the result of some deterministic force or a deity that has agency over our destinies? Does "fate" have some sort of agency? Or are we just like random randomness? Is everything we are and experience and who we were and who we might become, just "meant to be"? Do we have to live with the hand dealt to us? And I reckon that some of our categories don't really fit this conversation. For example, you can be a theist (believe that deity/God exists), but take a "watchmaker" posture. God wound up the laws of the universe and now it is just winding down like a big clock without God's involvement at all. This is Deism (if you want a fancy worldview word), which is what the founders of the United States were into. God had agency: God caused stuff to happen. But not too much. And only at the start. We want to be in control, but blame God for the stupid stuff we do. Deism is a great worldview for that.

Who or what is actually running the show then is a really important question. I would think that how you answer that question will shape how you make decisions, and particularly moral decisions. Will we own up to the results of our own choices, or pass the buck to fate, karma, God, gods, genes or some other force in the universe? How much free will do we actually have?

I'll leave you with that question, Kieren. I'll be out on the field next Thursday lunchtime again if you want to keep chatting.

Shalom, Mr Kemp.

Hi again Kieren,

Like you said in class, I think there is a link between free will and love. It's great to continue this conversation. We started it last week, remember, wandering around the field when I was on duty. In my previous letter, we asked the question "how free are we", actually? Or are we constrained, dictated to, harassed, cajoled, led by some impersonal or personal force in the universe? That conversation was triggered by ideas of karma which your classmates were arguing about, this idea that the results of our actions are inevitable: we are simply products of causes in a very long, even infinite, chain of causes. I get the question quite often, mainly from younger students. Year 9 students often come up with "if God is love, or full of love for us, then aren't we just all going to heaven anyway?" Hmmm. Interesting. I'm pausing here because even that question bumps up against the karma/freewill thing we were talking about: God has destined all humanity to go to heaven, so where's the free choice in that (even if the result seems attractive!). If God is obliged to let everyone into heaven, then maybe God is subject to the law of karma too? And we'd have to define what this "heaven" actually is (and can we be confident in whatever description we conclude)—even whether it's all that attractive. But that's another letter I think.

Anyway, free will and love. If God loves everyone, then God is sort of obliged to welcome us all into God's home—heaven—where that love can continue, no matter if we've been complete ratbags. We get this idea a lot with wobbly readings of the Bible. In terms of karma—this idea may actually break the cause and effect sequence (if it was justified to start with), because doing bad stuff does not necessarily lead to bad results: everyone gets into heaven. You'll share heaven with Adolph Hitler and Mother Teresa. But looking around at life, we do notice that doing good stuff also ends in a lot of crap sometimes. Remember Job in the Bible? And there are plenty of stories in the news of tragedies that happen to the most loving and righteous people for no apparent reason. There is a kind of ugly randomness to life that seems little linked to the moral character of people. Maybe it's a good thing that God welcomes everyone into heaven—if God does in fact do that (which we haven't established!). If you flick through the Psalms in the Bible you'll see that some of the writers are puzzled and get really angry with God for the good stuff that bad people enjoy and the bad stuff that good people suffer. It all feels a bit unjust sometimes!

Isn't it all just 'meant to be'

That may well be the point. I think we need to try and work through the very nature of love. The greatest definition of love—you'd struggle I think to find a better one across all of the world's literature—is the apostle Paul's definition in his first letter to the Corinthians (it's in the Bible). We sometimes read through it in class—maybe we should (it's chapter 13). But let's go back to creation accounts, and our own experience of being human. We read Genesis 1 and 2, and it's clear there that God creates everything good (morally pure, good quality, and fit for purpose). In Genesis 3, we read an alarming account where humanity (both male and female) decide to try and be like God—knowing everything, claiming omniscience, wanting to do stuff their way—and in doing this, we read God throws them out of the garden of Eden. This is an explanation why then so much ugliness follows in us down-the-line humans (us, even today). We read in those passages that God had created humanity for companionship, fellowship, for love. So hold that thought, and we'll pull in an example from today.

The key word here is "decide". Humans (Adam and Eve, if we allow they're two actual people) decide to follow the snake's temptation. They choose to try and be like God, believing that knowing everything is very attractive. God had created them with the ability to reject Him. And I think this is the key dimension of love: love is not just a feeling—warm fuzzies about someone awesome. God has created us to love Him, but we are not created as automatons, like robots with no free choice. It would not be love if we had to love. God has built into the universe a huge risk: we might actually reject Him, because love always allows this possibility. So then, perhaps free will is defined then as our ability, our choice, not to love God back, and even reject God completely. The seeds of this are explained in the stories in the first three chapters of Genesis. Simply put, the evidence that we have free will is that we can always say "no" even to love, or to the invitation to love and the offer of being loved. Truman chooses to leave the show, even when he discovered Christoph—the god figure in the film—offered him continued identity and destiny by keeping him in the show.

How Far Down Does the Elephant Go?

I had a conversation with Haley during the week, sitting on the railing outside our classroom. She reckoned we don't have free will, because look at advertising. She argued that we succumb to advertising so often and so convincingly that she thinks we tend to act because of subliminal messages being fed to us all the time, and we don't see them or know of them well enough to reject them. I certainly agreed that advertising is powerful—the advertising industry is right onto the psychology of persuading people to buy stuff and believe in things. The advertisers know how to appeal to our deepest longings, fears, desires, selfhood and identities. But we can still say "no". I told her I take real pride that I consciously reject the very things the advertisers want me to buy "on principle" I said. And she challenged me with a simple "really"? Well, maybe I have bought chocolate periodically because, well, the advertising that week persuaded me. (Am I rational enough to acknowledge that?)

In our most treasured relationships, love always has risk, and that's the whole point. We are free in our wills to choose to continue to put others first, and do all those amazing things Paul lists in 1 Corinthians 13. But we choose to love even though we can choose not to. We can choose to accept or reject God's love. We can choose to accept or reject our friends' and lover's love. If we couldn't then we'd be robots, right? And robots don't love. (Well in the emerging contours of AI, maybe they can. But that's another letter. We're talking about free will here. Alas, it all overlaps.) But coming back to the comment you hear periodically—"it was just meant to be"—I'm not convinced. I think we are created with a genuine free will to make choices that are real choices. We can make choices other than what our genes might program us for. Our lives could follow any number of possibilities, with any number of outcomes. And the argument from love I hope might be a useful example of this?

Hey, great chatting.
Shalom, Mr Kemp.

Isn't it all just 'meant to be'

Hamish,

It seems that you've had quite a discussion about karma. It triggered all sorts of wider conversations. Thanks for coming back to me—actually putting it out there to the class too—your question about determinism. It's a fancy way of asking the same question "is it all meant to be"? We've noted what might drive the universe—karma, fate, divine fiat (that is, God speaks and it happens), some sort of combination of time and opportunity like in Evolution, and there are a few other possibilities. But I know you guys debate the role of nature and nurture—I sometimes hear you in your groups particularly discussing whether people are "born that way" or whether we choose our behaviors. "He's just like that"—a sort of biological determinism. In parenting we hear the phrase, usually an excuse for cute, but bad behavior—"oh, boys will be boys"—explaining away why they fight, ogle the girls, or crash their cars.

This biological determinism is implied in the question we pulled from the box, directly pointed at me: "Sir, are you homophobic?" As I've assured you in the past, no question is too big to ask. So let's have a go at this: I'm "thinking aloud" as I write, as I'd appreciate your feedback (like with all my other responses too), and my thinking isn't well landed yet. My first response is as always, looking first at what we're actually working with, what's behind the question and what's the question actually asking. What does the word "homophobic" actually mean? I think the word gets tossed around rather liberally, usually loaded with more emotion than reason.

There is denotation and connotation to all words. First the denotation: what is the actual dictionary meaning, the breakdown of the components of the word? "Homo" is not to be confused with the "homo" of the name of our species "Homo-sapiens". There it just means "man". But in the context of what we've raised, the prefix we're working with comes from the Greek prefix "homos", meaning "the same". "Hetero" obviously means "different". The second part of the word is "phobic", from the Greek word "phobia", which means "fear, or fear of". So homophobic, the adjective, denotes (it's actual dictionary meaning), something like "the fear of sameness".

But we tend to use and understand what the word connotes. "Homophobic" means "anti-gay", pretty much, or something just as pejorative. It has social, personal, political, even religious meaning packed into it when people use the word. So when the question comes out of the box for me, the student is asking me: "are you anti-gay"? And in the context of me as a Christian Education teacher I'd guess it is muddled with all sorts of pre-assumptions about what Christians supposedly believe, like a sort of mass acceptance of exactly the same position for all three billion of us Christians on the planet. Our elephants are all standing on the same ground. So something like assuming—rightly or wrongly—that "since all Christians are anti-gay, then you, Sir, must be anti-gay too, right?" If we do reduce it simply to that interpretation, I'd want first to establish what exactly we might mean by the prefix "anti-".

So in short: I have no fear of sameness. I have no fear of gay people. And I'm certainly not "anti" them in any intentional shaming cancelling sort of way. And to my utter embarrassment, I admit that many Christians actually are, regrettably. But I do have a question lurking in the back of my mind. It's a question about what the elephant is standing on. And it's about determinism. And logic.

The proposition that I hear often is that "gay people are born that way". So they are gay because they can't help being that way. It is their destiny. Nothing they or you can do about it, and so the sooner they come out of the closet and we accept them, the better. There is a biological determinism that causes them to "be like this". So I may as well "come out and live my authentic self" and "be who I really am". Granted, this applies to heterosexuals as well. We are biologically determined by Evolutionary means—"It's in our genes"—and so I can't be anything else. I understand this claim is made right across the spectrum of LGBTQ+ as well.

But I find it quite difficult to build a good conversation at this point because there is a niggle. And this is the first time I've sat down and tried to write about it, to get some sort of order to the ideas sloshing around in my brain. And it's an argument from straight logic. It goes something like this:

Proposition A: in the biological order of things, a sperm needs to fertilize an egg to produce another human being. The sperm naturally comes from the male, and the egg from the female, and the egg is fertilized inside the female. We are formed in the womb, from one egg and one sperm. This means that a woman and a man have to be involved in sexual intercourse. They are both heterosexuals *ipso facto*.

Proposition B: Homosexuals don't have sex with humans of the opposite sex. A gay man does not have sex with a woman, by definition. That's what gay/homosexual means.

Conclusion: Therefore—and here's the end of the logic proposal—even if there is a gene for homosexuality, or a mutation for homosexuality (and nobody is claiming they've found one), it would not be passed on at all to the next generation, because homosexuals don't have intercourse with the opposite sex. In other words, homosexuals are not "born that way". Homosexuality cannot, by definition, be propagated sexually.

I'd quite like to know how a gay person might respond to this logic. Maybe I'm not seeing something. However, if in fact it's true, then we're still left with the question of why some people understand themselves to be gay. If they were not "born that way" then they must be gay for some other reason. What comes to mind naturally is that it is a choice they make. And if it is a choice, then biological determinism goes out the window, free will argument flies in, and we hold to the possibilities of ongoing choice, including that a gay person may choose to be straight.

And just another quick note here: because someone has homo-erotic thoughts, doesn't mean they are gay or that they are determined biologically to be anything other than straight. (There is a long conversation to be had here, perhaps in another context. I am a male adult human who grew up in a boarding school, and then also was a supervisor later in the same boarding school. I observed that boys between about 9 and 12 all have homo-erotic thoughts at some stage, but it is not necessarily a pre-cursor to coming out as gay. Most don't. It's perhaps better explained as a developmental phase?)

So I'd be keen to know what you think. Check my logic. It is a logic challenge to biological determinism. I suppose someone could claim to be gay for other deterministic reasons, like karma, fate, or divine fiat. But if we are to value and hold to free will, then I'd have thought one can always choose to "change your stars"—to use that great little phrase Will Thatcher uses in the film *A Knight's Tale* (2001). We are not necessarily determined to be who we are: it's not in the stars or our genes. We can always change. Genes we're given at conception do not necessarily determine ultimately who we are becoming.

Let me know what you think. We should keep talking about this in class.

Shalom, Mr Kemp.

11

"If God can do anything, then why doesn't he just fix stuff, like world hunger" and "What's this word 'shalom' you use all the time?"

Max,

I recognized your question on the whiteboard today: "If God can do anything, then why doesn't he just fix stuff, like world hunger". We were checking out that case study where people pray things, expecting God to give them stuff that, well, seemed rather trivial to you guys in class. Guidance for putting on a pair of socks in the morning? Getting a car park close to the football stadium? Surely God's got better stuff to do than pay that much attention to these details in our lives? And besides, God has given us a mind and free will to make those decisions for ourselves, right? Loved that you guys are debating these things in class. And I recognize that students who aren't Christians, or have no experience or knowledge of Christian ideas, think this type of expectation of God is, well, very presumptuous, if not a little absurd.

How Far Down Does the Elephant Go?

But if God can do anything, then he should be fixing the world, right? Looking at your question, it is close to the classic theodicy one: "if God is good why is there evil in the world"? Have a flick through that earlier letter and you'll see I've categorized that question as a moral question: is God good, and then, if so, is God responsible for the evil in the world? Your question is similar, but different. And I like that you recognize that by using the word "fix", you're acknowledging there's something broken about the world. And that's a good place to start, I think.

First: "if God can do anything . . ." I think you're alluding to God's awesome (and absolute) power—omnipotence. (We dropped in some of these big words into class—keep your vocab growing!) When we assume God can do anything, we're generally alluding to power, like God has huge muscles and can toss big stuff around, like planets. But secondly, you may be alluding to moral nature too: does "anything" include evil stuff (like when little children are starving through no fault of their own)? But the assumption we make here is that God being God can indeed do anything, do whatever God wants to do, well, because God-ness includes almightiness. I'd like to question this. Can God do anything?

At this point, people sometimes throw up mind-benders: "If God can do anything, can he make a rock that's too big for him to lift?" Students push this question my way every year, and some do it smugly like "gotcha". Like it's an impossible dilemma for God, therefore God doesn't exist or isn't powerful. Or something. But that question is like the classic Zen *koan*: "what is the sound of one hand clapping?" The question itself is not logically coherent. That's the point with Zen—it's supposed to break out of the bounds of language and logic. Our rock question also has logical problems with it, but it probably belongs more with Zen than Christian thought because of its deliberate linguistic knot. It's a question about language (syntax and logic), not about God.

But the sticking point is the assumption that God can do anything. That's the question: can God do anything? Another big word: ontology. It's really a question about being-ness (ontology). What is the nature of God and what are God's qualities of being?

IF GOD CAN DO ANYTHING, THEN WHY DOESN'T

If we say "God is good", then can we also say that "God can do bad stuff"? If we say "God is creative", then can we also say that "God is destructive"? When we say "can do anything", what does the "anything" actually include? So maybe it goes something like this: God—ontologically—cannot be untrue to His own character (morally pure, holy, for example), and therefore cannot act—is incapable of acting—in ways that contradict that nature. Can God do evil? No. Why? Because God would be acting then against his own character of holiness, purity, goodness, which ontologically he is incapable of doing.

Woah, I hear you say. God does lots of stuff that is "bad"—in the Bible there are plenty of stories where God brings destruction on people, or instigates wars or captivity, or solves some things using violence. Or at least, that's how some of the writers interpret the perceived actions of God in history. Some cynics argue that the "God of the Old Testament" is a God of violence and anger, but the "God of the New Testament" is a God of love, like they are two different gods, or that God has a split personality, or something similar. And what about the whole Jesus thing: you could argue that God deliberately sent Jesus to the cross, a heinous act of injustice, violence, child abuse! How can a supposedly loving God also be a cosmic bully (I've heard it said)? And these are honest and authentic questions. I too think about these things.

But I'm persuaded that some things that we read as violent, or even plainly evil, can be redemptive: God allows (causes?) some evil-looking stuff to happen when the payoff is a much greater good. Did God cause the evil? Are there different types of evil (maybe God's involved in some but not others)? Did God allow the evil for a greater good to follow? It's something I wrestle with, but I hold onto the ontological nature of God, that God is good and acts according to his own personality and character, to do only good. When we see bad, is it always God's action, and if it is, then is it redemptive? And is God's category of "bad" the same as ours? (That's back to the question as to whether all suffering is bad.) That's where I'd probably keep the conversation moving towards. (And remember: God's intervention with Israel—a special covenant people—does involve categories of violence we're uncomfortable with, like war and captivity. God is good but does bad stuff to Israel. But Israel is unique and bound by a covenant between herself and YHWH. Their God—YHWH—uses "evil", like foreign invasion, to teach and discipline Israel because of the covenant and the ultimate desire for good to come into the world through them ... lots here! And PS: any "evil" agent that YHWH uses, like the Babylonians, to discipline Israel, is itself still morally accountable to God for excesses in its actions.)

I think the second half of your question—"why doesn't God just fix things, like world hunger"—comes back to the Kingdom of God illustration I offered previously. God is in the process of fixing stuff (and yes the world is very broken), but in another time frame to what we expect (the in-between time of Jesus' first and second coming). And sometimes we're tempted to blame God for not intervening when it's our own stupid fault in the first place (world hunger!). Maybe God allows us simply to live with the consequences of our own stupidness and poor decisions? The consequences are the evil acts we see and experience. Would that make God untrue to His own nature? Maybe that would be God allowing us to be fully who we are—with a free will! We're free enough to do stupid stuff. We're free enough to accuse God of doing evil stuff.

Let's keep this conversation going.

Shalom, Mr Kemp.

Becky,

Thanks for reading though parts of the initial script of *How Far Down does the Elephant Go?* I appreciate your feedback, pushback and notes scribbled around the edges of the manuscript. I've taken the liberty of giving you the last word. Well, the last question, really. You noticed that I sign off my letters with the word "shalom" and you want to know why. Finishing with your question allows us to arrive at a temporary pause for this particular collection of unfinished conversations, but also sets us up for more conversation into the future. And there are plenty more questions on Postit stickers tucked away in several manila folders here on my desk.

Shalom is a word I've used for quite some years to finish any correspondence I've done, even right back to when letters—on paper!—were the norm. I've never quite known how to sign off a letter, and I've always sensed that an ending is really important: we attempted this with "yours faithfully" or "yours sincerely" on those old letters. With emails these days we go with "regards" or "cheers", or with the renaissance of Te Reo Maori here in New Zealand, we're trying to work in Maori language greetings and farewells now too. Text messages just end. We assume that the reader can see electronically who it's from, and we drop the niceties and get on with the business at hand!

So I've chosen to use the word *shalom*. It literally means "peace". In the context of a greeting (or a letter sign-off), it would be like a blessing. "Peace be to you." The word has been part of my life for a long time. You'll remember I grew up in India, and I did all my High Schooling at an international boarding school in North India, and the common greeting in our town was not in fact *namaste* but *salaam*. *Salaam* is a variant of *shalom*. You can track the words back to Persia and Arabia and Palestine and Israel. So when in the weekends when we could go into the city, or go hiking in the hills, I'd greet people with *salaam*. In essence, wishing peace to them. There is a lot of peace wished to each other in the foothills of the Himalayas in North India!

A couple of years ago I was travelling up north around the Hokianga Harbor here in New Zealand, and had taken accommodation for a night in an Airbnb and shared dinner with five other guests who were Israelis. Everyone ate together around a large table, and we had a really profound and meaningful discussion ranging over many important issues. Great food sourced from ocean, farm, and garden graced the table, supplemented by locally brewed cider and the best of New Zealand wine. As we gathered around the table, I heard modern Hebrew being spoken. The Israelis greeted each other and the rest of us with *shalom*. They used the word often throughout the evening. I concluded it was their normal default greeting, and in fact a sort of key-word that summarised their dreams and hopes. When you talk about Israel and her modern context, inevitably you have to use the word peace somewhere in the conversation. We all talked about peace a lot that evening.

Which is brilliant I think. In English the word *hello* feels a bit lame. What does it mean? It's just two sounds we say when we stand in front of someone the first time we meet them that day. "Hel. Lo". It doesn't even mean anything. Or if it does, perhaps something like "I acknowledge you're standing in front of me". If we said "Good morning" more consistently—"Good morning [to you]" is more explicit, and leans more towards a blessing. Or our common New Zealand greeting of "gudday", short for "Good day to you". But to greet everyone all the time—like my new Israeli bunk-room and dinner friends—with *shalom*, or "peace be to you", is well, just more meaningful. It's like a prayer. Muslims greet each other with "as-salaam alekum" (shortened, in my experience in north India simply to *salaam*) which means "peace be to you", and then you reply "wa-alekum-salaam", and unto you be peace [also]. In the Anglican Christian tradition, there is a section in the worship service where people turn to each other and "pass the peace". We say the exact words that the Muslim greeting has: "Peace be to you", and you reply something like "and also with you".

This is why I like the word *shalom* so much. And why I use it to sign off my letters. But what I want to convey is something deeper than just a cultural exchange, an "hello" between people. *Shalom*, or peace (in English) is a concept just about on every page of the Bible, certainly implicitly. And "peace" here doesn't simply mean the absence of conflict or warfare. You noticed this when you commented on my letter earlier about the differences between peace-keeping and peace-making. (Thanks for the positive feedback on those five lessons on peace-making, by the way.) Jesus calls his followers to be "shalom-makers", to intentionally intervene in conflict and initiate peace, and then build peace and then keep the good gains of living peacefully by prioritizing the practice of forgiveness and reconciliation. On Easter Sunday evening—the evening of the resurrection—the Gospel writer John records that Jesus greeted his hiding-away disciples with "Peace be with you", or if we examine the Greek, more like "Peace be amongst all of you".

There is something happening at a deeper level here. Jesus' peace is like a healing, a re-orientation, a new understanding, a comforting presence, a new context, a new community, with him at the center (like Mendez in *The Butterfly Circus*). If we zoom out to see this in the context of the whole Bible, *shalom* is something that the writers yearn for ever since it all unravelled in Genesis 3. God's *shalom* becomes the destination point of where all of history then heads. We could use the word "restoration": *shalom* would be a restoration of everything that God wants in creation, namely relationship between God and humanity, relationship with each other, relationship within each individual (our disfigured and contorted self), and relationship with the planet/cosmos. Pretty much everything that went wrong in Genesis 3. We've read this in class. Did you pick up on that four-fold consequence of Adam and Eve's rebellion in Genesis 3 that we unpacked a bit? (Well actually, *shalom* ultimately won't be a restoration of Eden. It's not a return to Eden. It's something grander, more whole, more alive, more God-present.)

And if we dig a bit deeper, we find that *shalom* is often associated with the idea of Sabbath. That's the 7th day in the story of creation when God rests. Sabbath rest is built into creation. (That's why we have a seven day week.) But Sabbath—for the Jewish people originally—was not just a day off. You don't just come home and blob for the weekend and go to the football and watch Netflix movies. Sabbath was an intentional time (starting at sun-down on Friday, going to sun-down on Saturday) where *shalom* was practiced, and lived out. Sabbath brings rest and peace, but it also pre-figured where the whole of God's intentional story was going. Celebrate Sabbath once a week and we are supposed to experience something of God's future, a deposit brought from that future into the present, here, now. God's promised re-creation of the universe (a "new heaven and a new earth") is a Sabbath-era of final *shalom*. Not just the end of warfare, violence, conflict, broken relationship (although of course it is all of this), but an intentional final bringing together of a new age of *shalom*-ness which includes intentional healing, restoration, and rest. A new age. Initiated with the resurrection of Jesus (D-day, remember?) and fully coming with the second coming of Jesus (VE-day, not yet happened).

I used to finish letters and emails with "cheers". Sometimes I forget and still do. But that's like being in the pub and toasting someone: "cheers and good luck to you". It's a bit lame. So I've moved to "shalom" at the end of my letters. I'm trying to condense everything that the Bible hopes for, that Jesus makes explicit: a true restoration of brokenness to healing, from conflict to restored relationship; a renewal of creation, from its groaning and twistedness to the full beauty of Eden and more; a resurrection—from death to new life; from a smoky and damaged lens to clear insights and enlightenment; new growth from the inner torments of despair, from broken identity and shattered dreams to hope and love—may all these be to you, today, in this moment and into your future in this life and the new Kingdom promised by God.

And so to answer your question, Becky, that is why I write *shalom* at the end of these letters and what I wish for all my past, current and future students.

Shalom, Mr Kemp.

www.ingramcontent.com/pod-product-compliance
Lightning Source LLC
LaVergne TN
LVHW021550080426
835510LV00019B/2463